General Editor:
Patrick McNeill

Family

Other books in the **Society Now** series

Adrian Wilson

FAMILY

ROUTLEDGE

First published in 1985 by
Tavistock Publications Ltd

Reprinted 1991, 1993, 1995
by Routledge
11 New Fetter Lane,
London EC4P 4EE

© 1985 Adrian Wilson

Typeset by Activity Ltd,
Salisbury, Wiltshire
Printed and bound in Great
Britain by Clays Ltd, St Ives plc

*British Library Cataloguing in
Publication Data*
A catalogue record for this
book is available from the
British Library

*Library of Congress Cataloguing in
Publication Data*
A catalogue record for this
book is available from the
Library of Congress

ISBN 0–415–06564–X

For Maggy

Contents

Acknowledgements

The author and publishers wish to thank the following for permission to reproduce copyright material: The Central Statistical Office for statistical material from *Social Trends*: Tavistock Publications for extracts from *Sex and Generation*; and the National Society for the Prevention of Cruelty to Children for permission to use the statistics and conclusions from *Trends in Child Abuse*.

Preface

The purpose of this book is to provide an introduction to the sociology of the family for the student new to the discipline. The family has not always been the most fashionable topic amongst students, although it continues to be one of the most popular areas for examination answers. I hope that this book will show students the range of issues and studies which comprise the sociology of the family, and will encourage many to explore outwards from the standard texts of the examination syllabus.

I would like to record my thanks to Diana Leonard who reawakened my interest in the family through her teaching in the Sociology Department of the Institute of Education, London University. Pat McNeill has provided all the patient support and encouragement that one could hope to receive from an editor. Above all I am grateful to Maggy for all her loving encouragement, and for her tolerance of the disruption that my writing has caused to our life.

Adrian Wilson

1

Sociology and the family

Sociologists are interested in the family for two main reasons. First, as individuals we are all members of a family group. Birth gives each of us a set of blood relations who surround us during our most formative years. Marriage brings us a new set of familial relationships. Such relationships may be dissolved through death, divorce, or distance.

The second reason for the sociological interest in the family derives from its central role in social life. The founding fathers of sociology, such as Durkheim and Marx, were interested in the way that the social fabric of nineteenth-century society was changing. The agricultural, industrial, and scientific revolutions were producing economic and political changes that threatened to create social chaos in Europe. The family was seen as one of the institutions that had to respond to these changes.

Concern with the family is not the exclusive preserve of the sociologist. Governments and politicians use the family as an indicator of the health and strength of social life. Politicians fear that any weakening of family life will in some way sap the vitality of national life. The introduction of the British welfare state was partly an attempt to maintain and improve the quality of family life. The family is also important to businessmen. It is one of the major purchasing groups of our consumer society. The basic needs of food, shelter, and warmth are usually met through the family. It is inevitable that much of our income is spent within the family. Any surplus income may well be used to provide the family with more comfort or pleasure.

The family is clearly an important social institution. But what is the family? Where do we draw the boundaries of our family? These fundamental questions must be considered before it is possible to take a more detailed sociological view of family life in modern Britain.

The changing shape of the family

There is no one definition or description of a typical or normal family. Broadly speaking, the family is a group of people related by blood or by law, living together or associating with one another to a common purpose, that purpose being the provision of food, shelter, and the rearing of children. The institution of the family keeps changing, and sociologists could describe a number of types of family that exist in a society at any one time.

Historical changes

The use of historical social science has shown that the family changes over time. Demographic factors have a key role in this process. Snapshot studies of the family at different points in history will show marked changes in such key indicators as age of marriage, fertility rates, and life expectancy. Authority patterns within the family, and an individual's expectation of family life, will obviously reflect the period in which they were born.

Studies show that our forebears had a very different view of family life from our own. Childhood is a clear example. The work of Philippe Aries (1962) shows that in the seventeenth century a child was treated as an adult, albeit a small one, from the age of seven. The child was dressed as an adult and was expected to work. But in the twentieth century full adult responsibility is sometimes delayed until a young person reaches their late teens or early twenties. The stages of childhood and adolescence that we take for granted are a relatively new development in the history of family patterns.

The family development cycle

Our own families change with time. Turner (1969) describes the development cycle of the British family, providing a framework for the examination of the way families adjust their form over a period of forty or fifty years. He suggests that there are four major reference points in the development cycle of the family. These are:

1 the public acknowledgement of the intent to marry;
2 the wedding ceremony;
3 the birth (or adoption) of offspring;
4 the dissolution of the family unit with the death of one member, which is completed by the death of the surviving partner.

The first phase can be described as the 'courtship' period. Casual friendships and dating start at school, and continue into the work or college stage. At some point a couple will move to a more serious commitment based on love. Our society still places great importance on the idea of romantic love, accompanied by the free choice of a marriage partner. The engagement ring is a powerful symbol of this commitment. Marriage marks the end of the courtship phase.

Marriage is one of the key events of life, the 'rite of passage' that marks the entry of the young couple into social adulthood. Diana Leonard (1980) shows that a proper wedding is a key

3

goal for many. Much time, effort, and expense are put into ensuring that the ritual of marriage is performed correctly. Leonard argues that marriage marks an important shift in the customary and legal relations between children and their parents. Marriage is one way of breaking free from parental controls. Couples move into their own home, demonstrating to the world at large their new-found independence.

The third phase is essentially concerned with childbearing and childrearing. It begins with the birth (or possibly the adoption) of the first child. Parenthood puts the young couple on a more equal footing with their parents. Our society expects a marriage to produce children. However, it must be remembered that about 10–14 per cent of married couples do not have children, a situation that can give rise to great sadness.

The childrearing phase can last anything from about sixteen to forty or more years. The length of this stage is determined by the number of children born to a couple and the time gap between births. Couples who have children early in their marriage may find that they are free of their responsibilities before they are forty, while others will still be supporting their children as they approach retirement.

Whatever the length of the childrearing phase, it must be stressed that it involves the parents in a prolonged period of very hard work. It is during this period that children receive their primary socialization into social roles, values, and beliefs. Both society and social scientists see this socialization process as being of the greatest significance.

The final phase in the family development cycle is the period of disintegration. This begins with the children leaving the home to set up their own families or households. If the couple had their children when they were quite young, then they may still have many years of marriage in front of them. Some adjustment in attitudes and roles may be required, particularly when they are faced with retirement. The increase in life expectancy which has taken place means that many more married couples will now live together for fifty or more years. The death of one of the partners begins the final breakdown of this family core. The remaining partner has to face the problem of living on his or her own, going to live with one of the children, or entering some kind of residential home for the elderly.

It is clear that this model of a family development cycle will not fit all families in modern Britain. Couples will start their families at very different ages and at different points in their marriage. Parents with only one child will experience family life in a different way from those who have large families. Those individuals who do not marry, and those couples without children hardly fit the pattern at all. Divorce will also interrupt the cycle of family development, forcing family members to alter their expectations and to create new households.

However, the study of the family development cycle teaches us one very important point. The family is not a static body, it alters and adjusts as the family members experience the different stages of life. The sociologist is faced with the problem of describing families that are always in motion. Sociological studies of families are often simply snapshots of that family at one point in the cycle of development.

Cultural differences in family forms

Family forms also vary according to the traditions and culture of particular societies. It is important that the sociologist avoids an ethnocentric view, that he or she does not judge other family forms as inferior to those in our own society. A number of examples of family types is given in this book. All are seen as natural and suitable by their members. Each is a product of a particular culture at a particular time in history.

Anthropological studies are a very important source of information on different patterns of family life. Social anthropology developed separately from sociology, and is concerned with the study of small-scale societies with cultures very different from our own. It is not only the study of what appear to be exotic forms of behaviour. Much of anthropology is concerned with the everyday features of life: birth, marriage, death, the cycle of family life.

Some of the most widely read studies are probably those of the American anthropologist, Margaret Mead. She started her field studies of Pacific Island cultures in the 1920s. Her two best-known studies, *Coming of Age in Samoa* (1943) and *Growing Up in New Guinea* (1963), give very clear accounts of the way young people in these societies are involved in family life.

In *Male and Female* (1962), Mead uses evidence from seven Pacific Island cultures to show the very wide variety of family roles that could be found. The Latmul of New Guinea had a noteworthy culture, with magnificent villages and large dwelling houses. The strong artistic culture had to be supported by a sound economy. It was the hard work of the women in growing sago, and in fishing, that provided the steady food supply. The mountain Arapesh had a much more meagre food supply. Harsh economic reality led to both sexes working alongside each other in growing food. Among the Tchambuli it was the women who were confident, energetic, and hardworking. The women fished and went to market, leaving the men to carve, paint, and practise their dance steps. The Mundugumor women were as assertive and vigorous as the men. They did much of the work, assisted by young boys, working sago, fishing, and collecting coconuts. The women detested the whole process of childbearing.

Mead's work provides a clear and easily read source of information on different family styles. It is a warning against judging other family systems by the standards of our own time and place. But it must also be remembered that these cultures have changed too. The fieldwork for these studies was completed over fifty years ago. These Pacific communities have been through a period of great change resulting from war, the process of modernization, and the impact of western culture.

The sociological analysis of the family

It is clear that there are many problems facing the sociologist studying the family. The family is an institution that changes in shape and form, appearing in different ways to different people. However, certain themes and issues are of particular importance. It is therefore possible to construct a framework for the study of the major issues affecting the family.

Studies of the family commonly deal with three aspects of family structure. These are the significance of kinship in modern industrial societies, the functions of the family, and the changing roles within the family.

Central to all three of these themes is the notion of change. From its earliest days sociology has been concerned with how social institutions such as the family have changed with the development of the modern, urban, industrial society. Some sociologists have argued for a 'march of progress', with the family refined into a more complete and successful form than in the past. Such a debate over the changes in the family must also lead to a consideration of the ways in which sociological theory affects our view of the family.

The significance of kinship

Membership of a family involves us in relationships with those people we see as kin. Our kin are those people who have a family relationship with us because of links of blood or marriage. Running through all these relationships is some sense of obligation. Sometimes these obligations have legal force, for example, in parent-child relationships. But more commonly they form part of our shared 'taken for granted' assumptions about family life, the feeling that children have a debt of obligation to their parents.

The sociological question is to try to determine where this sense of obligation weakens or stops completely. It may help to view family relationships as a social network of contact and significance. At the centre of the network there may be frequent contact with relatives, and these relationships may be given great significance. Further out, on the fringe of the network, are relatives that are hardly ever seen and are remembered only by Christmas and birthday cards. Some relationships may be weak simply because of the physical problems of distance. An uncle or aunt down the road may be given more significance than an uncle or aunt in Australia. But it is not only distance that weakens relationships. Family feuds and personality clashes can lead to a break in contact. Many families lose contact with sons or sisters, or even parents, even though they may still live in the same town or community.

Sociology has used two models of family structure to help the analysis of kinship. These are the 'extended family' and the 'nuclear family'. Almost inevitably students new to the subject give these terms an almost sacred status. It is often assumed that the extended family existed in Britain before the industrial revolution, and that it was then replaced by the nuclear family. Such a simplistic view is not supported by the sociological evidence.

The extended and nuclear family models should be seen simply as analytical tools that can be used in the study of kinship relationships. They can be described in ideal-type form to give a focus for comparative study. It is unlikely that they will ever exist in pure form in our society. Indeed, much of the sociological debate over kinship is concerned with the meaning of such terms as 'the modified extended family', 'the isolated nuclear family', or 'the privatized family'. Nevertheless, it is important, if only for examination purposes, that students know the difference in meaning between the two terms.

The extended family is distinguished by a wide range of kin who may live and work closely together. The needs of the whole family group may be seen as more important than the wishes of the smaller groups within it. The child growing up within the extended family learns to accept the authority of the oldest members of the family. Marriage is a matter for the whole family. It involves both economic and emotional obligations to another extended family. It is not the free choice that we expect for a young couple in love. For a man, the duties he owes to his kin may be as important as his obligations to his new wife. There are many studies which show the problems of the young wife marrying into the strong family group.

The nuclear family is a much smaller unit. The central core of the nuclear family is the relationship between husband and wife. Their marriage and the creation of a new household unit may mean cutting some ties with the wider family. The nuclear family is created by the arrival of children who become the major responsibility of the family. Where the nuclear family predominates, society is made up of a series of separate two-generational households.

These definitions should be taken as a guide for analysis, not as a description of family life in Britain. Too often sociology students try to argue that the evidence of studies clearly shows a movement from extended to nuclear forms of the family. In particular, the early work of Peter Willmott and Michael Young (1957, 1960) has suffered as generations of students try to force their evidence on London families into the appropriate mould.

Studies of the British family show a wide range of types. Every modern society will have a variety of family forms. Later chapters will try to draw some conclusions about the structure of these contemporary family forms.

The functions of the family

A second major area of interest has focused on the functions that the family performs in and for society. The family is seen to play a key role in helping the individual to learn the social behaviour required by society. Such an approach is rooted in one major sociological theory, that of structural functionalism.

Functionalism is concerned with the overall structure of society and the processes by which social institutions work together to maintain the structure of that society. The family is seen as one of the key institutions binding the individual into the fabric of social life, a universal body which serves the same functions in all societies.

9

There are certain key functions that the family performs. In the first place the family provides society with an orderly means of reproduction, while at the same time the norms of marriage control the potentially disruptive forces of sexuality. Second, the family provides physical and economic support for the child during the early years of dependence. The child receives its primary socialization in the family, learning the essential ideas and values required for adult life. It is at this time that the child learns some of the traditions and culture of the society into which it is born. Through the socialization process the child will learn the patterns of behaviour expected in certain social roles, for instance, gender roles.

The adult finds both economic and emotional support in the family. Economic rewards may be seen to be distributed and consumed through the family. Our society's notion of romantic love provides the emotional support that allows an individual to cope with the stresses and strains of adult life. Functionalists would argue that the core functions of the family (reproduction, socialization, economic and emotional support) are to be found in all forms of family structure – that they are universal.

There may be other functions which are considered of lesser importance. Various studies have looked at the way in which the family has had educational, political, or religious concerns. Others have looked at the family as the major centre for leisure and recreation. The growth of the modern state with its highly developed welfare services is thought to have taken away some of these non-essential functions, leaving the family free to concentrate on the essential functions of socialization and the stabilization of adult personalities.

The family is seen by functionalists to have a crucial role in maintaining stability in society. Functionalists have therefore been interested in the way in which the family has adapted to the forces of industrialization and urbanization. Other studies have focused on the pathology of the family, the possibility that the family might break down under the pressure of modern living. Underlying both of these functionalist concerns is the assumption that the family has and should continue to have an essential and positive role to play in society. This has led some functionalists to argue that the nuclear family is unavoidable, as it is well suited to the modern world, a claim that will be examined later in this book.

Changing roles within the family

The socialization process within the family prepares us for some of the basic social roles which the individual must play. The family moulds our identity and the development of our personality. It is therefore not surprising to find that sociologists have been concerned with the changing role relationships within the family.

There are three key role relationships within the family: the child-family relationship, the husband-wife relationship, and the role of old people. Each one has changed markedly over the last two hundred years, and each is subject to the influence of changing demographic patterns, increased prosperity, and new attitudes to family life.

The most dramatic change in roles may be seen in the child-family relationship. Ariès (1962) showed that childhood as we know it hardly existed in the Middle Ages. Children were mixed with adults as soon as they were capable of some independence. The young child soon played an economic role in the family, starting with the simplest tasks around the age of seven and later assuming more responsible roles. The working child was an economic necessity for many poor families. It was only in the eighteenth century that a more enlightented view of childhood began to develop, and then only for children from the most prosperous families.

The nineteenth century saw a number of changes that altered the nature of childhood. The most dramatic feature was the increase in the life expectancy of children and the improvement in their health. Public health measures and developments in scientific and medical knowledge meant a better chance of survival into adulthood. At the same time the efforts of social

11

reformers removed the youngest children from the workplace, and developed a system of compulsory full-time education. The extension of the school-leaving age has tied the child to the family for a much greater period. Economic and social factors have led to smaller families, allowing parents to give more attention to their children.

Ariès saw childhood as a relatively brief period. Today childhood and adolescence occupy a major part of our life. It is almost impossible to say when a young person can be seen as an adult. The school-leaving age is set at sixteen, but you cannot vote until the age of eighteen. Many people still see twenty-one as the start of adulthood. What is clear is that young people now make up a significant proportion of the population. In 1981 there were 12.1 million children under the age of fifteen in Britain, just over 22 per cent of the population.

The extension of childhood allowed the creation of a youth culture, or rather, a range of youth cultures which allows a young person to find knowledge, entertainment, and an identity outside the family. Parents have had to adjust to a post-war generation of young people with a markedly different outlook on life from pre-war teenagers. The post-war generation now has teenage children of its own. Changing attitudes and experiences have sparked off a large number of sociological and psychological studies of youth culture, adolescence, and the problems of young people.

The changing role of young people in the family contrasts vividly with the experience of the growing numbers of elderly people who are becoming isolated from their families. Studies of traditional societies show how old people are respected for their wisdom and experience. By contrast, our society increasingly sees the elderly as out of touch and in the way. Increased life expectancy and better welfare and medical facilities have led to a large increase in the number of old people. Ermisch (1983) shows that the increasing numbers of elderly people will cause major problems for society in the early part of next century. A smaller than ever proportion of the workforce will be struggling to support the dependent population of both young and old.

Many families now face the problems of coping with elderly members. Inevitably these demands will be met with mixed feelings. An old person may seem a nuisance if they are living with a family in a relatively small house. Equally, the old person may deeply regret the loss of independence that frailty brings.

The popular view is that modern families no longer offer the dependent elderly the care that they once did. However, Parker (1982) points out that studies show that families give immense amounts of assistance and support to elderly relatives. Much of the burden of this care falls on the wife. Parker points out two complicating issues. First, many wives now return to work when their children go to school. Their income is often essential to the family economy. In this situation can the family afford to help an elderly relative? Second, there are many old people with no relatives. Age Concern estimates that perhaps a third of old people have no family members who can help them. In either of these two cases, the burden of care for the elderly may have to fall on the local authority.

It is not unfair to observe that sociologists of late seem to have neglected the role of old people in the family. The fashionable sociological concern has been with youth culture. The elderly have been labelled a social problem and handed over to the social worker. The one exception to this neglect are the feminist sociologists who have noted how often the caring role descends on the shoulders of women.

The third area of sociological interest has been the role relationship of husband and wife. Much of the research has taken the form of community studies, where the changing roles of husband and wife can be located in the wider social life of the community.

Studies of urban working-class families suggest that husbands and wives have segregated roles. The husband's major role is that of breadwinner, while the wife looks after home and children. Many community studies observe that the relationship between mother and daughter is particularly strong, a union of women based on an exchange of services at critical periods of family life.

Sociologists have been interested in what marriage and childbearing mean for women. Early research such as Myrdal and Klein (1956) looked at the problems created for women by the attempt to combine family responsibilities with paid employment. Gavron's (1966) study of ninety-six north-London mothers explored further the significance of combining work with family roles. She suggested that while working-class wives worked largely for extra money, middle-class wives returned to work for the social contact. Rapoport and Rapoport (1976, 1978) took this research one stage further with their studies of dual-career families and working couples. Such family structures create emotional and practical problems for the married couple, but particularly for the wife.

Feminist research in the 1970s has given sociology further insight into the position of the woman in the family. Oakley's studies (1974a, 1979) of housework and motherhood have raised questions about the role of men in the family. Most recently there has been a series of studies of fatherhood, for instance Jackson (1984), in an attempt to develop our understanding of the male family role.

Two examples of alternative family structures

This chapter has provided a framework for the analysis of family structures by the use of the three concepts of kinship, functions, and roles. The analysis can also be applied to family structures which are very different from our own. The Nayar of southern India and the Oneida Community of the United States provide us with two historical examples of alternative families.

The Nayar of Kerala

Anthropological interest in the Nayar of Kerala in southern

14

India centred on whether they were a true family system, or a possible exception to the belief in the universality of the family. Gough (1959) studied the Nayar form of marriage as it was in the eighteenth century, before the impact of British rule.

The Nayar family group consisted of brothers and sisters, together with the children of the sisters, and their daughters' children. They formed one economic group, owning or leasing property together. The oldest male, the Kāranavan, was the legal guardian. The warlike Nayar men trained as soldiers, spending part of each year as hired mercenaries. Only the Kāranavan, the women, and the children remained in the villages. The Nayar developed a family form that could cope with the instability of such a system.

Each kinship group was linked by hereditary ties of ceremonial co-operation. The pre-puberty marriage rites of Nayar girls were particularly important. Girls below the age of puberty – those between the ages of eight and twelve years – were ritually married to men from linked kinship groups. Sexual relationships only took place with girls close to puberty. Ritual bathing cleansed the pollution of cohabitation. The ritual husband then left and had no further obligation to his bride.

The bride did not live with her ritual husband. Her only obligation to him was that she and her children observed the mourning rites for him on his death. The ritual marriage was important for the girl as the rite of passage which opened up the sexual and maternal roles of adulthood.

The young Nayar women entered a very unusual form of marriage. The woman took a small number of visiting husbands from the surrounding neighbourhood, perhaps between three and eight in all. The husband gave his wife gifts in return for the sexual relationship, but in no sense did he support her. Food and clothing came instead from the matrilineal group.

When the woman became pregnant it was essential for one of the visiting husbands to acknowledge that he was probably the father. He did this by giving cloth and vegetables to the midwife who helped at childbirth. The 'father' was then freed of any obligations to, or social rights over, the child. Children were brought up and socialized by their mother's kin group.

The Nayar were an interesting family grouping that lacked the central 'nuclear' element which is so powerful in contemporary families. Husband and wife relationships were downgraded in significance. But this family structure clearly worked. Kinship retained its importance. The basic family functions of reproduction, sexual control, socialization, and economic and emotional support were all performed.

The Oneida Community

The second example of an alternative family structure is almost more surprising than that of the Nayar. The Oneida Community was founded in 1848 at Oneida Creek in central New York State. The main founder was John Humphrey Noyes, a perfectionist Christian preacher who believed in creating the Kingdom of God on earth. Life was to be based on spiritual, economic, and sexual equality.

The Oneida Community attempted to put these beliefs into practice, pursuing economic communism, group marriage, sexual equality, and scientific breeding. The community of several hundred members were all housed in one large building, although each adult had his or her own room. The building and community life were fused together.

Oneida was a community of action. The members erected their own buildings, grew their own food, made their own clothes, and ran a community laundry. Children were taught in their own school. All the activities at Oneida were designed to emphasize the 'we' rather than individual desires. Dancing and card playing were allowed because they brought people together, but the use of alcohol, tea, coffee, and tobacco was resisted, because this was seen as individualistic and appetitive in nature.

Religion was central to the community, providing a unifying force and social control. Any member who caused problems was brought before a committee of peers for a frank discussion. This system of mutual criticism seems to have been well accepted, survivors testifying to a remarkably stable and happy community.

Two features of Oneida marked it out as a unique family structure – a form of group marriage, and a programme of eugenic breeding. Oneida's system of marriage was based on the belief that members should all love each other. Members did not live as couples. A man wanting sexual relations with a particular female member would make his approaches through an older, respected member of the community. That person approached the woman, who could accept or decline the approach.

We lack the detailed historical information to know how this system worked. For instance, did the women make such advances to men? What is clear is that however unusual this system of sexual relations, Oneida remained a very moral community. Coarse and suggestive behaviour were not allowed.

Oneida distinguished between sexual activity for procreation – the production of children – and sexual activity for recreation. Noyes had been impressed by theories of evolution, and decided that Oneida should introduce the scientific breeding of children. Reproduction was controlled by using coitus reservatus, sexual intercourse up to but not including ejaculation. The young men of the community were expected to learn such sexual control with the older women, while the men introduced the young women to sexual relations.

This system of controlled breeding was known as stirpiculture. Fifty-three women and thirty-eight men were considered to be physically and spiritually suitable as parents or stirps. In ten years fifty-eight children were born in this programme, although a few other children were born by mistake.

Children were looked after by their mother for the first fifteen months of their life. They were then moved into the children's section of the community house. Oneida made a conscious effort to play down any sentimental feelings of affection between parent and child. All the adults in the community were expected to treat all children as if they were their own.

The community grew to several hundred members, but pressure from the authorities and the local churches led to the collapse of Oneida. The members were accused of irregular sexual activity. Noyes fled to Canada. The community broke up in 1880. A business enterprise survived the collapse, with the stock shared among the remaining members of the community; it is still possible to buy Oneida cutlery in British shops.

The Oneida Community fits our pattern of family structure. The functions of a family were provided. Children grew up to learn social roles. Biological relationships were replaced by strong social obligations. Oneida was clearly a deviant form of family structure, but it was a community which seemed to work.

Activity

It is possible to learn a great deal by studying your own family. Parents and grandparents can provide a vivid picture of family life when they were young. Some families have traced their roots back over many generations by consulting parish records. Try to reconstruct a picture of the way that your own family has changed over the last one hundred years. You can also learn a great deal from talking to your friends or fellow students who come from different ethnic backgrounds. Is family life for them very different from your own?

Further reading

Harris (1983) gives a good account of the sociological approach to kinship, marriage, and the family in the first part of his book. Morgan (1975) is more theoretical, but his book is worth studying; the second chapter 'Why kinship?' explores the sociological interest in the theme. Gordon (1972) gives some interesting insights into alternative patterns of family structure.

2

Theoretical approaches to the family

Sociology has a number of theoretical traditions. Theories that emphasize the importance of social structures have had a powerful influence on the development of the discipline, but have been challenged more recently by approaches that place the emphasis on the individual act. The sociology of the family reflects the full range of theoretical perspectives, as will be shown in this chapter. Later chapters will show how these theoretical approaches are used in actual studies.

The functionalist approach – is the family good for society?

Functionalism came to dominate sociology in the 1940s and 1950s, particularly through the work of the American sociologist, Talcott Parsons. Sociologists were concerned to find the means by which society remains stable. Functionalist sociology developed a framework of ideas which outlined the major social systems of the society, and the links that exist between these social systems.

The family was seen as one of the core elements of the social system, providing a crucial link between the individual and the wider social group. Any change or decline in the family would have a major impact on the whole social structure. Functionalist sociology, with its optimistic faith in the evolution and progress of society, was able to mount a strong defence of the post-war American family against charges that it had been severely weakened.

Functionalist sociologists developed an analysis which showed that the family had evolved into a superior form. Studies by Murdock, Goode, and others were able to show that the family, in changing its form, had been left free to concentrate on the most important functions. Parsons (1956) saw the two most important functions to be the socialization of the young and the stabilization of the adult personality.

Central to the debate over the functionalist view of the family is the notion of 'fit'. The isolated nuclear family was seen to be a good 'fit' for post-war American society. The family had been left free to make a good job of rearing the children, with more 'professional' parents working alongside teachers and childcare experts. The family was also able to concentrate on the demanding relationship between husband and wife. The family provided both the child and the adult with the physical and emotional support needed for their roles in society. It also provided the motivation to be successful in an industrial world which laid stress on achievement by individual effort.

The functionalist account of the positive role of the family in society coincided with a period of strong public support for the American family. Berger and Berger (1983) argue that this was a period when the American family was seen as a success, particularly in the way it placed the needs of the individual at the heart of family life. The child-centred family was seen as progress. Women were allowed to find purpose in family life, in the expressive roles of mother and wife. The man's emotional needs were to be met in his instrumental role of breadwinner. The modern family was therefore a good fit for

21

modern society, serving both individual needs and the requirements of the broader social system.

The functionalist approach supports the 'march of progress' view of the family, the idea that the family has reached its most advanced stage of development. The progressive evolution of the family is implied in Parsons's work rather than clearly spelled out. Indeed, one of the major criticisms of functionalist studies of the family is that they are ahistorical, that they lack a proper historical perspective. Functionalists seem to describe the family form as it is and then imply that, because it exists in that form, that is how it should be. Not surprisingly, functionalists also failed to see how the family might develop in the future.

The 'march of progress' view is essentially an optimistic statement of faith in the evolution of the family. This can be seen clearly in Fletcher's (1966) defence of the contemporary British family. He used historical sources to show that there was no golden age of family life in the past. Rather it was Fletcher's belief that the moral and social improvement of society had created a stronger and more functional British family.

Fletcher argued that the family still had five key functions. First, it regulated sexual behaviour. Second, it provided a responsible basis for the procreation and rearing of children. Third, it cared for its dependent members, whether young or old. Fourth, it was the earliest and most powerful socializing agency. Finally, it taught family members the roles they would play in society, helping them accept the rights, duties, and obligations linked to these roles. His work suggested that the British family had never been stronger.

The contemporary British family was seen as a success. Fletcher gave the definitive functionalist description of the British family. It was:

1 of long duration, since it was founded at an early age;
2 small in size because it was consciously planned;
3 separately housed in an improved material environment;

22

4 economically self-responsible, self-providing, and independent of wider kin;
5 founded and maintained by partners of equal status
enjoying a marital relationship based increasingly on
mutuality of consideration;
6 democratically managed in that husband and wife, and
frequently children, were all taken into account in family
decision-making;
7 centrally concerned with the care and upbringing of
children;
8 aided in achieving this health and stability by a wide range of
public provision, both statutory and voluntary.

Fletcher's approach seemed to be supported by the evidence
of many of the community studies of family life, for instance
the work of Willmott and Young (1957). It is, however, a
model that has been much criticized over the last two decades.
The functionalist approach has given an oversimplified view of
relationships within the family, especially in relation to the role
of women. The model also fails to allow for the great variety of
family forms which exist in every society. This oversimplified
view plays down the influence of social differences based on
class, status, religious, regional, or ethnic background.

However, the functionalist view has provided a significant
framework for a comprehensive view of family life. Second, it
generated a tremendous amount of research material, mostly
in the positivist tradition, which still forms the basis of much of
the comparative study of the family.

A feminist approach – is the family good for women?

Feminist research has provided one of the most wide-ranging
critiques of the functionalist view of the family. Women have
been involved in the campaign for greater sexual equality
throughout this century. The 1960s saw the growth of an
organized feminist movement. Feminism was, in part, a
reaction against the cult of domesticity which had been so

23

powerful in post-war America and Europe. The publication of Betty Friedan's *The Feminist Mystique* (1963) helped to bring together some of the strands of ideas and hopes that have become the basis of the women's movement.

Feminism spread to Europe in the late 1960s, helping to raise the self-awareness of many women of their own social position. The move towards greater sexual liberation and the development of the gay movement were also attempts to reconsider some of the basic social attitudes of society. A parallel movement tried to make people aware of the problems of racial prejudice, and to raise the self-consciousness of ethnic minorities.

It is important not to fall into the trap of claiming that there is one feminist movement, with only one feminist viewpoint on any issue. The movement is a coalition of attitudes, beliefs, and needs. Even the commonly used distinction between radical and Marxist feminists is too simple. What does unite women is a common concern over a series of issues.

Feminists have begun a close examination of the place of women in history and in society. Consideration of the domestic role of women has a central place. The changing role of women in society has created both practical and political problems in obtaining equality of treatment with men. The debate over the role of women has spread into education and to the media. Some women have had their self-consciousness raised in such a way that it must have altered their whole experience of life.

Sociology has been greatly influenced by the development of a feminist perspective. Oakley (1974b) has pointed out that women were invisible in much of traditional sociology. Much of the sociology about women was written by male sociologists from a male point of view. The criticisms put forward by feminism have led to the rethinking of many key areas of sociology. In particular, the sociology of the family has been revolutionized by the insights provided through feminist research.

A feminist sociology of the family requires the student first to re-examine the history of our society, most of which has been written by men. Male historians were largely interested in what men said and what men did. This has made it appear that women were largely excluded from political, economic, and cultural life. Even social historians have underplayed the role of women by concentrating on the industrial and economic life of men. History has, therefore, given us a limited view of the world, a view which has ignored the experience and understanding of women. Feminism has encouraged historical research by women. This new history of the other half of our world has produced many new insights into the role of women in society.

Oakley (1974a) has provided one of the most readable accounts of the historical changes affecting women in the family. She shows that before industrialization women played a major economic role within the family. This historical perspective allows us to understand the development of sexual divisions with the growth of an industrial society. In particular, it raises the question of how and why, in nineteenth-century Britain, it was seen that the rightful and natural place for a woman should be at home.

The second major area of interest for feminists is the allocation of roles within the family. The historical evidence shows that women's role both within and outside the family changes over time. Feminist sociologists have also been interested in the way the role of women varies from culture to culture, and also within any society. Anthropological evidence has been used to show how sex roles vary. Studies in Britain show that women from middle-class backgrounds use their greater educational expertise to develop a wider range of roles. The professional middle-class woman has probably achieved greater freedom than any of her working-class sisters.

For most women, marriage and motherhood will be the dominant events of their lives. Housework and childcare continue to be predominantly the sphere of women. A feminist approach to the family asks why these roles are seen almost exclusively as women's work. The family socializes young girls into the traditional gender roles. Women are trapped by the

25

patriarchal family, which is dominated by the demands of the man.

A Marxist approach – is the family a tool of capitalism?

Marxism has had a major impact on the development of sociology. Within the Marxist approach is an account of historical development, a theory of social class, and an analysis of capitalist society. Economic relationships are considered to be the central force that drives the development of a society, while at the same time they are also the means of keeping control over the members of that society.

An account of the evolution of the family was given by Friedrich Engels in *The Origin of the Family, Private Property and the State* (1884). The book borrows evidence from anthropology to show that there was a series of stages in the evolution of mankind. Social institutions, such as the family, changed in form alongside the changes in the nature of economic subsistence.

The earliest family forms were communistic households where women were seen as equal to men, although there was certainly a sexual division of labour. The domestication of animals and the cultivation of plants marked a major economic development. Men took control of this new source of wealth. Power and status went to the man. Property was passed from father to son. Man's work was seen as the most important, while the work of women was no longer seen as socially significant.

The main problem with the writings of Engels is his failure to describe the origin of the sexual division of labour. He did not examine how the patterns of sexual divisions developed and who benefited from them. Instead, Engels drifted into a biological explanation which implies that women do the tasks which are natural for them. He also failed to point out that the technological relationships which affect the family are all under the control of men. The result is that Marxist theory failed to explain the sexual division of labour and its significance for women.

26

What Engels was able to show was that the family was not a fixed institution. It changed over time. Changes in the social relations of production changed the family. Engels also showed that women often had an inferior place in the home, that they were domestic slaves.

For many years Marxists largely ignored the family as a political and social issue. It was believed that any faults in the family would be corrected by the creation of a socialist society. The revival in the Marxist theory of the family came with the examination of the issues raised by feminists about the nature and causes of sexual inequality. At the same time, Marxist academics were writing about the detailed economic and social controls that exist in capitalist society. The importance of the family as part of this process of social control was quickly recognized.

There has been a major debate between Marxism and feminism over the nature of the work that the woman does for the family. It is often referred to as 'the domestic labour debate'. Writers have argued that the capitalist economy needs to have women working in the home. The housewife services the needs of her husband, feeding and comforting him so that he can go refreshed to work each day. In a similar fashion, the mother ensures that the young children of the community are brought safely through childhood to become workers in their turn.

Women are also part of what Marxists have called the 'reserve army of labour'. When the economy booms there is a need for more workers. Many women are available to be brought into industrial work as required. This was clearly illustrated by the way women were recruited into the factories during two world wars. Women have a second economic advantage to capitalism: they are cheap labour. Women are not seen as chief breadwinners of the family, therefore they can be paid a lower wage.

The 'domestic labour debate' is still continuing. Marxists have yet to resolve the precise way in which the labour of women fits their economic model. Nor have they really explained why domestic work and childcare have to be reserved largely for women. Feminists point out that it is not only capitalism that benefits from having women doing domestic work, it is also men! Those who recognize both sides of the debate have to cope with the problem of changing capitalism at the same time as improving the position of women.

There is less argument over the role of the family as part of the process of social control. This is not a new idea in sociology. Functionalist sociology has a very strong emphasis on the family as the main agent of socialization. Marxists recognize this role of the family but, unlike the functionalists, do not see it as beneficial. The family transmits the dominant bourgeois culture of capitalist society, preventing people from seeing the world as it really is.

One of the clearest accounts of this approach can be seen in the work of the French Marxist, Louis Althusser (1971). Althusser's work on the way in which the state achieves social control clearly locates the family in what he calls 'the ideological state apparatus'. The state does not need to use physical force to control people. If it can control what people believe, then they will co-operate with a government dominated by the ruling class. Education, religion, the media, and the family are all central elements of the ideological state apparatus. The population is controlled through the socialization process, by what they come to learn and believe.

The Marxist sees the working-class family socialized into a state of false consciousness. The small family encourages its members to think in individual terms, to try to obtain what is good for the family. In doing this it weakens the bond between the man and his working-class brothers. At the same time, the comfortable, welcoming home is a distraction for the worker. It helps the man relax and forget the problems of his position at work. The family becomes the psychological haven that weakens the workers' determination to stand and fight capitalism. The family, according to the Marxist, becomes an obstacle to the revolution.

28

The radical psychologists – is the family bad for the individual?

The fourth theoretical view of the family is associated with a group that has been labelled the 'radical psychologists'. The key figure is Ronald Laing, a psychologist who became a cult figure in the 1960s. Laing and his colleagues were interested in the development of the 'self', the inner core of awareness in each of us. Their main theme was that the family could damage the development of individuality by providing an environment that was too restrictive.

Laing sees a dark, dysfunctional side to the family. Relationships within the family are often confused. Love is matched by anger, jealousy, and shame. Tension and hostility that exist between husband and wife get passed on to the child. Powerful triangular relationships form an emotional battleground. The child has an identity thrust upon it, rather than being allowed to develop a free personality.

Much of Laing's work is based on his study of schizophrenic patients. Madness, according to Laing, is one way that some individuals use to escape the conflict that is inherent in family life. There is always a psychological tension between the dependence of a child on its parents, and the child's progression to an independent adult existence. Parents want to see their child grow up, and yet they want to hang on to the small dependent child. Such tensions can be expressed in a number of ways. There may be physical violence. Alternatively, one of the family members could become 'mad'. A mental disturbance such as schizophrenia can be seen as one way of resolving or escaping from the tensions that a child experiences in the family.

David Cooper (1971) adopts a similar approach to Laing. He argues that the family destroys the inner life of a person, by preventing the free adoption of the 'self'. Family relationships based on love trap us in such a way that we are unable to be ourselves. Rather than being a creative environment for the child, the family destroys the chance of an independent existence. The child develops self-other dependencies rather than living for itself. The child gets taught a role, rather than being allowed to choose to develop as he or she wants. Family members develop a need for love, which as well as bringing some pleasure, becomes the basis for repression, violence, and guilt.

The work of the radical psychologists has given sociology important insights into family life. It is a counterbalance to the optimism of the functionalist view. This approach shows the significance, and the complexity, of the psychological relationships within the family. Feminists have also picked up this theme, looking at what the family does to the self-image of women. Both the radical psychologists and the feminists look for a break with conventional family life as a way of allowing the individual to go free.

Support for these critical views of family life comes from the anthropologist, Sir Edmund Leach. In 1967 he gave the annual BBC Reith Lectures, creating a great stir with his attack on the modern family. He supports the radical psychologists in their belief that there is too much privacy in the family. The family has become too inward-looking. Modern housing has distorted family life. Houses are now too small. The family has shrunk into itself, cutting itself off from the wider world. Two quotations from Leach sum up this critical approach to the family:

'It is not that we have too little privacy – we are compelled by our housing arrangements to have too much .... Come what may, the English will continue to rear most of their children cooped up in boxes like battery hens. They have no choice.'

(Leach 1982)

'Today the domestic household is isolated. The family looks inward upon itself, there is an intensification of emotional stress between husband and wife, parents and children. The strain is greater than most of us can bear. Far from being the basis of the good society, the family with all its tawdry secrets and narrow privacy is the source of all our discontents.'

(Leach 1967)

Sociological theory and the study of the family

Two points need to be made as a conclusion to this chapter. First, it would be wrong to try to draw sharp boundary lines between the various theoretical approaches to the study of the family. There are links and shared perspectives between these different approaches.

Second, one theoretical approach has not been mentioned in this chapter, interactionism. The interactionist sociologists are essentially concerned with the internal workings of the family, a micro approach. Their studies look at processes such as courting, at the meaning of marriage, and at parent-child relationships. Many studies of the family are interactionist in form, but have their origin and location in a Marxist or feminist perspective. The sociology of the family has clearly benefited from the cross-fertilization of different theoretical viewpoints.

Further reading

Harris (1983) and Morgan (1975) again provide the basic sources for further reading. The functionalist approach to the family is discussed by Harris in terms of the 'fit' between family and society. His book also gives a clear account of the Marxist analysis of the family in capitalist society. The second half of Morgan's book gives a sophisticated analysis of the work of Laing, and of the place of women in capitalist society. Delamont (1980) gives a more down-to-earth account of the sociology of women. Finally, Berger and Berger (1983) cover the whole of the theoretical debate in their own fascinating, if eclectic, style.

31

3

How to study the family

Sociologists use a range of research techniques to study the family. Both positivist and interpretive methods are used. However, most pieces of research into the family use more than one method of data collection. Many family studies use qualitative material as illustration.

There are both ethical and moral problems in studying the family, for it is one of the most private areas of our lives. Sociologists investigating family life need to be aware of the emotional sensitivities that can be revealed by our investigations. Feelings of pride or inadequacy may lead respondents to cover up their real feelings, or to put a different gloss on their factual answers. The gender of the interviewer may well affect the kind of answer which is given to a question.

The family is a small group, which makes it difficult for the sociologist to use observation as a research technique. The presence of a sociologist in the kitchen, living-room, or bedroom would clearly inhibit normal family life. Sociologists are therefore forced to place great reliance on the more formal techniques of interviewing and external observation.

This chapter considers three styles of research into the family. The first example draws on the work of Willmott and Young to show how large-scale survey techniques have been used to trace developments in family structure. The second looks at Leonard's work on marriage in Swansea as an example of more qualitative research conducted by one person. The third approach looks at some of the demographic tools that are used to study the family. More specifically, this approach looks at the use of historical social science as a means of revealing the history of the family. All three examples combine the use of quantitative and qualitative methods, but each has the stress on a different approach.

The classic survey studies of Willmott and Young

The studies of family and community by Peter Willmott and Michael Young must rank among the most widely read works of British sociology. Their surveys formed part of a series of studies published through the Institute of Community Studies, an independent research organization founded in 1954. The studies undertaken for the Institute were an attempt to apply the strengths of anthropology to sociology. Their distinguishing feature was the combination of the personal observations of the researchers with the statistical analysis generated from social surveys in particular communities.

Three studies by Willmott and Young develop the theme of the changing post-war British family. The earliest, *Family and Kinship in East London* (1957), was a study of the impact of rehousing schemes on working-class families from Bethnal Green. The second study, *Family and Class in a London Suburb* (1960), was an attempt to discover whether a middle-class suburb, Woodford, had a different pattern of family life to the new working-class suburbs such as 'Green-leigh'. Both these studies reflected a methodological alliance between sociology and anthropology. The third study, *The*

Symmetrical Family (1973), linked the sociological research to a historical perspective.

Survey techniques were used in each of the studies. The quantitative material produced from the surveys provides much of the evidence for Willmott and Young's generalizations about family life. Each of the studies was centred on a general sample of men and women which reflected the social mix of the community in which they lived. Specialist samples were then used to investigate particular aspects of family and community life. The main surveys in each of the studies are listed below.

'Family And Kinship in East London'

1 The General Sample: 933 men and women were asked a series of fairly brief, standardized questions. This sample provided the bulk of the statistical material for the study.
2 The Bethnal Green Marriage Sample: 45 couples who were married with two or more children under the age of fifteen. This group was interviewed fully and provided most of the quotations and individual accounts which are used in the study.
3 The Greenleigh Marriage Sample: 47 couples with two or more children under the age of fifteen, who had moved from Bethnal Green to Greenleigh. They were interviewed twice, with a two-year interval to provide accounts of changes in family life following the move to Greenleigh.
4 The Grammar School Sample: this was a small sample of women who passed through local grammar schools in the five years 1935 to 1939. It provided some information on social mobility, but the authors were very wary of its reliability given only 24 respondents.

'Family and Class in a London Suburb'

1 The General Sample: a random sample of 939 people drawn from the electoral register for Woodford.

2 The Old Age Sample: a sample of 210 old people in Woodford. The sample was drawn from the records of six local doctors. It provided evidence on the family experience of the elderly.

3 The Marriage Sample: this was a sub-sample of 44 married people, with at least two children under fifteen. The marriage sample allowed the authors to make a comparison with the Bethnal Green study.

'The Symmetrical Family'

1 The Main Sample: this was made up of 3,000 people representing a cross-section of the London Metropolitan Region. They were selected from 24 local authority areas. Only 1,928 were interviewed, a 64 per cent response. The information was transferred from questionnaires on to computer tapes. A particular analysis was made of the relative influence of class, car ownership, and other factors, on the range of leisure activities.

2 The Sample of Active Sportsmen: the authors were interested in the relationship between sporting interests and family life. Fifty-one people were interviewed, men predominating, with a relatively large proportion of managers among them.

3 The Managing Directors Sample: 190 male directors were interviewed to provide details about the family life and working life of a prosperous section of the middle class.

4 Case-Studies of Firms: this was a small study of staff in an electronics firm a few miles outside Greater London, and a glue factory in Inner London. A further study was made of two establishments operating shift systems, a post office, and a printing firm.

5 The Time Budget Study: 411 individuals completed diaries that provided a guide to the time they spent on family, personal, work, or leisure activities.

The surveys provided Willmott and Young with a framework of quantitative data on which they could build their hypotheses. Inevitably they were faced with all the problems of supervising such large-scale research. The three pages of acknowledgements at the start of *The Symmetrical Family* show the size of the research team. The authors name 52 interviewers, 14 coders, 8 typists, as well as a number of supervisors, advisors, and other specialists. The research data was contained in over 6,000 tables; 55 tables appear in the main text of the study with a further 19 in the appendices.

The study faced the usual methodological problems associated with quantitative research. The surveys had to be planned carefully in order to produce accurate data. The interviews on family life needed to be based on a representative sample. Interviewers had to be trained, sent out, and supervised. Information from the inverviews had to be coded and transferred on to computer files. The quantitative data had to be analysed, material had to be selected, and the key findings prepared for publication.

Although Willmott and Young are working within the positivist tradition, their studies do not make dry reading. Their quantitative data is balanced with more qualitative material. Those interviewed were allowed to speak for themselves, describing their family life in their own words. The work of Willmott and Young represents much of what is best in the tradition of community studies.

There are also problems with this approach to the study of the family. These studies are essentially snapshots of family life at particular periods. They are limited to one geographical area of Britain during a period of twenty years. To what extent is their data valid for the rest of the country? What significance does the quantitative data have for the wider sociology of the family? Unfortunately, many students fail to see beyond Willmott and Young, continuing to believe that Bethnal Green is still typical of British family structures. The result is that the significance of Willmott and Young has been distorted because they have assumed the status of modern sociological classics.

'Sex and Generation' (1980) – a qualitative study

This study of courtship and marriage by Diana Leonard is clearly different from the large-scale studies of Willmott and Young. Leonard believed that studying the rituals associated with courtship, getting married, and setting up a new household would give her important insights into the nature of family relationships. Like Willmott and Young she was working within the traditions of British social anthropology. The wedding ceremony was the 'window' that allowed Leonard to observe the relationships of one town in the late 1960s.

Leonard's research is a good example of the qualitative approach that can be adopted by one person working alone. Swansea was chosen because that was where she was living at the time. The interviewing was to be done unaided, in the evenings, when she could make herself free of family commitments. The fieldwork was spread over a long period. The study commenced in 1967, with the interviewing taking from autumn 1968 to autumn 1969. The research was not published in book form until 1980. Leonard argues that it took her a long time to think through her research material and to build it into a theoretical framework. She also points out that the delay was partly due to her being a female sociologist engaged in primary research. It was necessary for her to get away from the pressure of being a wife and mother before she could get the time and motivation to finish her study.

Unlike the survey methods of Willmott and Young, Leonard was solely concerned with gaining qualitative insights into the significance of marriage. Marriage involves an important shift in the social and legal relationship between parents and their adult children. Leonard wanted to uncover the elements involved in both courtship and marriage. The large-scale survey was seen to be inappropriate. The actual process of research allowed Leonard to develop her ideas on the issues involved. The theoretical framework, with its strong feminist

37

perspective, came some time after the stage of information gathering.

It was Leonard's intention to contact about fifty couples. She wanted to interview them before their marriage, to attend some of the weddings, and then call back for a second interview about six months later. The second interview was designed to explore how the couple felt about their wedding, and also to observe how the couple had set up home. Extra information was to be obtained by interviewing the bride and groom separately, and by talking to both sets of parents. Information about the ritual of marriage was to be obtained by talking to the shopkeepers, the caterers, the clergy, and the taxi-drivers who were all involved in the organization of weddings. Diana Leonard even attended some marriage preparation classes, an unusual example of participant observation.

One of the particular problems that Leonard faced was actually obtaining the details of weddings in her chosen research period. The superintendent registrars needed some persuasion to release details of forthcoming marriages, even though such information is meant to be open for public inspection. It also took time to get the clergy to respond to written requests for details. However, she did obtain a final sample of thirty-four church weddings and twenty registry office weddings.

Courtship and marriage have both very public and very private elements. Researchers working in this field must take care that they do not overstep the boundaries of what is seen as acceptable questioning. Diana Leonard found it helpful to be a woman. Those being interviewed found it 'natural' that a female sociologist might be interested in courtship and marriage. Conversely, being a woman meant that she could not see some men on their own, weakening her insight into the way men felt about their forthcoming marriages. There were times when Leonard felt that some of the men were being sheltered from her interviewing.

The nature of the subject matter helped to determine the form of the interviewing. Leonard used semi-structured interviews with a schedule of questions to ensure that she obtained essential information. But she also wanted to make her interviews as conversational as possible. The interviews took almost two hours to complete. The interviewing took place in the respondent's home, allowing her to observe the family environment of her interviewees.

The results of her interviews, together with her own observations, provided her with a wide range of data about the ritual of marriage. She now had accounts of courtship and engagement. The contents of 'bottom drawers' had been revealed to her. She had had the chance to observe at first hand the symbolism and rituals of hen parties, weddings, and receptions. All this qualitative information enabled Leonard to achieve her initial research aim which she had stated as:

'When I started this research I was concerned to provide a description of a particular phase in the development cycle of the domestic group, and I was especially interested in showing what the associated ceremonial was saying about the structures and implicit values.'

(Leonard 1980: 286)

Leonard had shown how courtship dominates the lives of young people, and that it was important to marry 'properly'. Her research also showed the great complexity of the ceremonial rituals that surround marriage. However, *Sex and Generation* is more than simply a description of courtship and marriage. It is an example of the way that the process of research generates theoretical insight. Leonard writes: 'Only later, after the experience of the fieldwork, did I come to analyse the material in terms of inter-sex and inter-generational relations in a particular socio-historical context' (Leonard 1980: 286). She was able to present her research findings within a feminist perspective which showed the need to recognize that the basis of marriage is a labour relationship.

A woman is under considerable social and economic pressure to marry. But courtship and marriage reflect an unequal sexual relationship. A woman cannot take the initiative in courtship. The rituals of marriage reflect the domination of the man. The reality of married life is the role of the woman as the unpaid provider of sexual and domestic services to the man. Leonard argues that the ceremonial associated with courtship and marriage simply confirms that marriage is essentially a labour relationship, even though it is shrouded in love.

The methodology of historical social science

Historians and sociologists are often thought to be dismissive of each other's discipline. Sociologists have condemned the narrow view of some historical studies, while historians have dismissed the sociological tendency to make generalized statements. In fact, there is a great deal of common ground between history and sociology.

Both historians and sociologists are concerned with the social and cultural context of their research. The particular individual or institution does not exist in a vacuum but is influenced by the surrounding social world. Historians and sociologists are influenced in their choice of study and their method of approach by their own individual and cultural backgrounds. Each discipline has been guilty of ethnocentric bias, judging institutions in the light of personal experience.

It is in the field of methodology that history and social science have now come closer together, particularly in relation to the study of the family. The Open University has coined the term 'historical social science' as a way of describing this collaboration between the disciplines. Historical social science is the application of historical data to the social sciences. The key sub-disciplines that are involved are historical sociology, historical geography, and economic history. The techniques of historical social science have been used to improve our understanding of the demographic patterns of the last few hundred years.

Demography is the study of population trends. The study of demographic trends is important in itself, but it is also important as an essential tool for the analysis of changes in family structure, changes in fertility and in mortality rates. These changes have major implications for the family.

The population of a particular society is the result of the balance between birth and death rates, and of patterns of migration into and out of that country. The analysis of these patterns allows demographers to chart the age structures of societies, and to work out the rate of growth or decline of a particular population. Such information is vitally important for governments which have to plan the production and distribution of resources. Gomm (1981) has pointed out how demographic information provides a knowledge base for state policy and, at the same time, represents an individual's relationship to the state. Demographic categories, when attached to an individual or a family, become 'official status markers' which help determine large packets of rights and obligations in a welfare society.

The key demographic variable for sociologists is fertility. Hawthorn (1970) sums up the issues in one basic question. How many women have how many children over what period of time? A whole host of factors is involved in providing the answers to this question. At what age do women become capable of becoming pregnant? When do women get married, and does this correspond with the start of their sexual activity? How fertile are the women of a particular age, or at a particular period in history? Is any form of birth control used to limit fertility? What proportion of women do not marry, or do not choose to have children?

Official statistics express fertility in a number of different ways. It is not very helpful to be told simply that about 629,000 children were born in 1983. The figures need to be put in some kind of comparative form. There are a number of statistical measures of fertility which are used to allow comparisons to be made.

1 The crude birth rate: this measure shows the number of births per year for every 1,000 people in the population. The figure for 1983 was 12.7 per 1,000 (England and Wales).

41

2 The general fertility rate: this links births to the number of women of childbearing age. It is defined as the number of births per year per 1,000 women aged between fifteen and forty-four. The figure for 1983 was 59.7 births per 1,000 women aged fifteen to forty-four (England and Wales).

3 The total period fertility rate: the official definition from the Office of Population Censuses and Surveys is as follows, 'The total period fertility rate is the average number of children which would be born per woman if women experienced the age-specific fertility rates of the period in question throughout their childbearing life-span.' In 1983 the total period fertility rate was 1.76 children.

The crude birth rate is not that useful, except as an indication of general trends. It must be remembered that the figure includes men, women, and children of every age in each unit of 1,000 people. The general fertility rate gives us a better picture of trends. The total period fertility rate is useful in that it indicates trends in family size. The somewhat complicated definition is simply an attempt to show what the average family size would be if current fertility rates were applied to the childbearing period of a typical family. A population that wishes simply to replace its numbers must average just over two children per family. The 1983 figure of 1.76 therefore shows that if current fertility rates continue, the average completed family size will be below replacement level. The significance of these fertility rates for family formation will be discussed later in this book.

Demographers are also interested in how long we live. Deaths are measured in a very similar way to births. Mortality rates are expressed in terms of the number of deaths per 1,000 people per year. The early years of life are particularly vulnerable, so there are specialized measures of mortality for young children. The perinatal mortality rate is the number of stillbirths and deaths in the first week of life expressed as a rate per 1,000 live and still births. This figure can be compared with the infant mortality rate, the number of deaths in the first year of life expressed as a rate per 1,000 live births. It is obviously possible to work out a mortality rate for any age group.

Peter Laslett's *The World We Have Lost* (1965) marks a breakthrough in the development of historical social science. Since then, the Cambridge Group for the History of Population and Social Structure has built up a huge bank of data based on 750 parish registers. The information covers baptisms, marriages, and burials since 1538. This bank of data represents the largest body of historical demographic material anywhere in the world. Sophisticated statistical techniques now allow us to look backwards through history at the structure of the family in earlier centuries.

It is not necessary in this study to go into the detail of techniques such as family reconstitution, or back projection. Sociologists have used these techniques alongside more traditional secondary sources such as letters, journals, and official reports. Laslett (1983) provides the clearest example of this approach, combining demographic data, historical sources, and a sociological analysis of changing family patterns in England.

Conclusion

A good grasp of sociological methods is important for the understanding of the sociology of the family. It must be remembered that most sociologists are going to use more than one methodological approach. Feminist sociology is a good example of this mixed approach. Sociologists within this perspective have used almost all methods, from the most quantitative to the most qualitative, to throw light on the position of women in society.

Further reading

The best way to gain a good understanding of how to apply sociological research methods to the family is to look at some of the classic studies. Willmott and Young include a description of their methodology in each of their books (1957, 1960, 1973). Read the whole of Leonard (1980) to understand the range of methods that can be used to study everyday aspects of family life such as courtship. Bell and Newby (1971) give a good review of community studies as a method. Any of the works of Laslett (1965, 1977, 1983) will show you how the techniques of historical social science are put into practice.

4

Changing British families

It is widely believed among sociology students that in the period before the Industrial Revolution, the dominant form of family life was the extended family. Michael Anderson (1980) traces this notion back to the work of the nineteenth-century French sociologist, Frederic LePlay.

LePlay describes a model of a stem family which was common in the rural areas of Europe. Agriculture provided a stable way of life, with the peasants tied to their land and community. The family was strongly patriarchal. The eldest son assumed the family responsibilities when his father became too old or died. The household was usually limited to the patriarch and his wife, one married son and his family, and any other unmarried children of the head of the household. Such a family might have up to eighteen members. This stem family is the basis for the belief in a stable self-sufficient extended family.

The work of LePlay also provided for an unstable family form that might be more typical of urban industrial communities.

This family was much smaller and did not have the deep roots of the extended family. It was created by the marriage of two individuals and lasted only for the time it took to work through one family life-development cycle. As the children became adults, starting their own families, the unstable family would fade away. This unstable nuclear family was seen as the pattern for the future.

The work of historical social scientists has presented a radical critique of the model put forward by LePlay. Central to this critique is the work of Peter Laslett and his colleagues, together with members of the Cambridge Group for the History of Population and Social Structure. An impressive data bank of comparative material has been built up through the study of the records of 750 English parishes. More recently comparative studies have been made of communities in Europe, North America, and even Japan.

The pre-industrial family

In *The World We Have Lost* (1965) Laslett is mainly concerned with rural English life in the seventeenth century. Industry and agriculture existed in a symmetrical relationship. Many families survived through cottage industry, with work put out by merchants to be done at home. Industrial work in the home was often combined with casual labour on the land. This economic structure lasted until industrialization brought the factory system.

Laslett uses data from parish records to demolish a number of myths about the pre-industrial family. First, he says that there is little evidence for the existence of marriage at an early age, a feature which could account for the presence of extended families. He points out that girls reached maturity much later than today, and those from poor families might not become capable of childbearing until they were nineteen or twenty years of age. Today many girls enter puberty before their teens, the result of a rise in living standards and a better level of nutrition.

46

Marriage took place at a relatively late age. Laslett suggests that the average age of brides in the Elizabethan and Jacobean periods was twenty-four years, and for bridegrooms twenty-eight years. The late age of marriage, the relatively low level of fertility, and a low life expectancy would all combine to reduce the childbearing phase of family life. This would seem to suggest that the widely held belief that the pre-industrial family was large was a second myth. The evidence in *The World We Have Lost* seems to show that household size remained remarkably constant at 4.75 persons per household from the late sixteenth to the early twentieth century.

The high level of infant mortality meant that the average life expectancy in seventeenth-century England was in the low thirties. However, a man who reached the age of twenty-one might expect to live for another thirty years. If he married in his late twenties he could expect to enjoy about twenty years of marriage, but he would probably not live to see his children marry. The high mortality rates of the period meant that every community had a large number of widows, widowers, and orphans. People at that time were used to living with bereavement. Families were not multi-generational: Laslett argues that only about one household in twenty contained more than two generations. Grandparents were relatively rare compared with today.

Society was overwhelmingly youthful when compared to modern Britain. The evidence from several communities suggests an average age of about 25.4 years. Seventy per cent of households contained children. This youthful population had to support only a small proportion of old people, an interesting comparison with modern Britain where the elderly (those over sixty-five years of age) make up one in seven of the population.

In a later work, *Family Life and Illicit Love in Earlier Generations* (1977), Laslett suggests that there was a family form that was found widely in western Europe. The study used the records of sixty English communities together with twenty from Europe. The same pattern of family structure was found in England, northern France, and other north-western European countries.

There were four characteristics of this family form. First, it was predominantly a nuclear family. Second, women married and had their first child relatively late in life. The figures from seven English communities suggest the following age at marriage: 1550–99 24.9 years, 1600–49 25.9 years, 1650–99 27.0 years, 1700–41 27.2 years. The late age of marriage reduced the likelihood of three-generation families. Third, the age gap between husband and wife was small; indeed about a quarter of the wives were older than their spouses. Fourth, a significant number of households contained non-kin, often domestic servants. Something like 40 per cent of all children became servants in their teens or early twenties. Service was a stage in the life-cycle of many young people.

Laslett is careful not to make too sweeping a claim for his model of the western 'ideal-type' family. He does not maintain that it was universal at all times and in all areas of western Europe. It was not possible to draw neat maps dividing Europe into different patterns of family types, although it is clear that parts of the Mediterranean, and of central and eastern Europe had a family form much closer to LePlay's stem family.

It is now twenty years since the publication of *The World We Have Lost*. The work had a major impact on the way sociologists viewed the development of the family. Laslett has returned to that study (1983), and argues that most of his hypotheses about the family have proved accurate. Perhaps most important of all is the confirmation that life in pre-industrial Britain revolved round the nuclear family. Reproduction, socialization, work, and welfare were all based on the family. Industrialization arrived to shatter this world – it was the family world that was lost.

The family, industrialization, and change

The agricultural and industrial revolutions which started in the eighteenth century had a major impact on the social fabric of

Britain. The period 1750–1870 not only saw great technological change, it saw major demographic changes as well. There was a rapidly falling death rate while at the same time the birth rate remained high. Fertility was largely uncontrolled. More people were being born than were dying. The result was a population explosion. The population of England and Wales in 1760 was 8 million; by 1851 it had jumped to 21 million.

The enclosure movement in agriculture and changes in farming practice pushed surplus labour from the country to the towns. At the same time the growth of the factory system created new job opportunities in industrial areas. The period saw a strong flow of migrants from rural communities to the expanding towns of industrial England. Sociologists have tried to explain the effect that these developments had on the structure of family life.

Michael Anderson (1980) argues that there are three significant approaches which have been used to explain the changes in family patterns. The first, the demographic approach, has already been seen with Laslett's work on the pre-industrial family. Changes in the age of marriage and in fertility continue as the family adapts to industrialization.

The sentiments approach offers a second way of looking at change in family life. Anderson sees this as a concern with fundamental changes in the social relationships within a family. The writers within the sentiments approach have used qualitative data rather than the quantitative data of the demographers. Evidence gathered from diaries, contemporary writings, religious tracts, and literature is used to study the changing attitudes within the family. Studies such as Ariès's (1962) show how the family moved away from a relatively emotionless open unit dominated by male attitudes to a growing emphasis on affection, privacy, and individualism. The family began to be seen as a source of pleasure and happiness, both for the married couple and their children.

The third approach to family change is the household economics approach. Anderson says that this kind of explanation involves a concentration on the economic behaviour of the members of the family. The key questions are, how does the family support itself, how does it handle family resources, and how are these passed on to the next generation? This is particularly important for families in the country. Every peasant family had to have enough members to work the land, but not too many to eat up all the food.

The relationship of parents to children was also an economic one. The parents had to secure the future of their children, but also try to prepare for their own old age. The sexual division of labour was crucial. A wife had an important economic role as she could work in the dairy, help on the land, or prepare materials for the home weaver. Children were also expected to earn their keep. Older children might go off to work in domestic service or find employment as seasonal labour.

Anderson's (1971) study of family and household structure in Preston, Lancashire shows the significance of economic forces. The study was based on the analysis of data from the 1851 census. It showed that during the growth of Preston as a cotton town, there seemed to be an increase in the proportion of households in which parents lived with their married children. Anderson argues that there was an increase in co-residence because of the advantages to both parents and married children.

In the cotton towns family income could be increased considerably if the wife also worked in the mill. This could be achieved if relatives, often the parents, were brought into the household to care for the children. Anderson has set up an exchange model where the obligations of kinship can also provide the best economic reward. The household gains a higher standard of living, while the parents have both support and a role in their old age. Rather than the family becoming more nuclear with industrialization, Anderson has provided us with an example of a move towards the extended family structure.

The family in Victorian Britain

Victorian Britain is often seen as a period of stability following the upheavals of the industrial revolution. It is also portrayed as the era where the family as an institution was at its strongest. Politicians still call for a return to the Victorian family values of thrift and discipline as an answer to current social problems. But what was the Victorian family?

The first and most important point is that there was not one Victorian family. Smelser (1982) argues that family forms varied between and within social classes. Social status distinctions were very real in Victorian Britain. There were clear status differences among the wealthy, between members of the aristocracy, industrialists, and those in the professions with respect to education, attitudes, and life style. The working class was split according to levels of skill and standard of living. Country people lived in a different world from those who lived in the towns and cities.

The aristocratic family was likely to be bigger than its lower-class counterparts. Wealth isolated the rich from many of the pressures of the real world. A family house in London would be matched by a country estate. A visit to any of the larger National Trust properties shows the sheer size of these country houses and the huge number of domestic servants needed to run them.

The male members of the upper-class family were not only concerned with their estates, they were often a major force in local and county politics. The aristocratic woman was left to cultivate her manners and her artistic talents, with perhaps some involvement in local charitable work. Leonore Davidoff (1973) has given a fascinating insight into the social round of the 'best circles' and how a complex set of rules of etiquette grew up to govern the London Season.

Smelser argues that the middle-class family was dominated by the role of the man as head of the household and as sole provider. The result for the middle-class woman was the 'emptying out' of her family role. Marriage and motherhood dominated her life. The wife was responsible for maintaining the order of the household, and she created order by being an example to her children, to the household, and to men. The middle-class woman became a specialist in leisure, developing

51

skills in music, sketching, and letter-writing. Her sexuality was denied, as it was for children and servants. Davidoff (1976) describes the middle-class family as a 'domestic idyll', a haven against the evils of society.

The whole edifice of Victorian middle-class respectability rested on double standards of sexual morality. Women's sexuality was denied, while male sexual licence was met by prostitution on a scale that sharply contradicted the public morality of the day. Ronald Pearsall (1969) gives a vivid account of the world of Victorian sexuality. Men of all ranks used prostitutes. London in the 1850s had over 5,000 brothels. Child prostitution involved girls as young as twelve. Pearsall's evidence hardly recommends a return to Victorian sexual values.

Middle-class women faced problems if they did not marry. The unattached woman with no income was a liability to her family. Finding a husband was a common theme in nineteenth-century novels. One of the few acceptable roles for the unmarried woman was that of governess, but this was poorly paid and lacked social status.

However, changes were in sight for the middle-class woman. There was the slow growth of education for girls, and a quickening interest in what was a suitable curriculum for them. A few girls from middle-class families moved into higher education, and the fight began to get women accepted into professions such as medicine. On the social class boundary between the middle and working classes, new job opportunities appeared. The growth of teaching and nursing gave middle-class women new horizons.

The working-class family had a very contrasting life style. Working people, whether in industrial city or isolated village, lived very close to the edge of economic disaster. Illness, unemployment, industrial disputes, or economic slumps could plunge families and whole communities into poverty. There was no safety net of a welfare state to help the family facing poverty. The choice was often between help from relatives or the austere regime of the workhouse. The workhouse was designed to be an unattractive place, an end to be avoided if at all possible. Every member of the working-class family worked hard to make ends meet.

Women worked in a wide range of jobs, from mining to textiles to farming, and work was combined with the cycle of family life. Girls might start their working life in factories or domestic service. Marriage and childbearing interrupted this process, but women needed to find some way to supplement the family income. In the country, women helped with the harvest or did seasonal jobs such as fruit picking. Young girls from Scotland followed the herring fleet, gutting and packing fish on the quayside. On top of all this, women continued to be responsible for cooking, cleaning, and childcare.

Children were also expected to work. Many of the jobs in the mines and the factories involved great physical effort, or even danger to the child's health. The domestic role of children was just as important. A young child could be left in charge of younger brothers and sisters, freeing the mother for work. However, the nineteenth century saw a move by enlightened opinion to remove women and children from the worst of the factory jobs.

The earliest Factory Acts tried to improve working conditions in the textile industries. In 1833 the hours of work for children under thirteen years of age were limited to nine a day, and twelve for those up to eighteen years of age. The 1842 Mines Act outlawed the employment underground of women and children under ten. Other Acts introduced a requirement of fifteen hours a week schooling for young people, and cut the working day to ten hours. It must be remembered, however, that these Acts applied to a relatively narrow range of industries. The extension of legislation to other industries and its effective enforcement took many more years.

The development of state education had a major impact on the role of children in the family. Some children had had a basic education in church schools, in ragged schools, or even in Sunday schools. The 1870 Education Act ensured that the school system would be expanded so that there were enough places for all children. The school-leaving age was gradually raised so that it stood at twelve in 1899. At the same time attempts were made to ensure that children attended school regularly. It was always a temptation for parents to keep their children away from school if it was possible for them to earn a little extra money.

Demographic and social changes at the turn of the century

The end of the nineteenth century saw a major change in family size. In the 1890s the infant mortality rate began to fall rapidly. The inevitable result of a rapid fall in infant mortality should be an increase in average family size, unless of course fertility is controlled. In fact we can see a fall in the birth rate from about 1870, a trend with major implications for family life.

Women who married in the 1860s averaged 5.7 live births. By the 1920s the number of live births per married woman was down to 2.2. There was also a marked decrease in the number of very large families. In 1860, 63 per cent of marriages produced 5 or more children. By 1925 only just over 12 per cent of families had 5 children. There was a corresponding increase in the proportion of small families. In 1860 a mere 5 per cent of families had only one child, but by the end of the 1920s some 25 per cent of families had a single child.

Sociologists and social historians have been interested to find the reasons for these changes in fertility patterns. A number of social and economic pressures have been suggested as explanations. Three particular factors need special consideration. These are the changing attitude to children, the increased use of contraception, and the changing role and status of women.

The changing attitude to children

We have already seen how there had been a change in attitude to the role of children in the family. Economic pressures also suggested that there were advantages in having fewer children. The 'utility' model of explanation says that the number of children in a family can be explained partially by their utility or usefulness. The running costs of children needed to be set against the benefit they brought to the family. The fall in infant mortality could have meant a big increase in family size. What would have been the utility of these extra children?

Children had become more expensive for both middle-class and working-class families. The social life of the urban middle class had become more expensive. The children of these families needed expensive schooling if they were to obtain the qualifications that had become necessary to maintain middle-class status. As a consequence, middle-class families concentrated their resources on fewer children. Working-class families were also under pressure to limit their families. They had lost the earning potential of their children with their exclusion from work and their compulsory attendance at school. It made equal sense for the working-class family to limit the number of children born.

There was also widespread official concern with the health and welfare of the population. The poor health of young men applying to join the armed forces led to a series of initiatives to improve the health of children. Academics were starting to take a more scientific view of child development. Higher standards of parental care were being demanded. The small family was seen as one possible solution to the problem of the quality of childcare.

The increased use of contraception

The fall in the birth rate that took place at the end of the nineteenth century was clearly related to the increased use of contraception. Birth control was not new. Historians have shown that many couples used coitus interruptus (the withdrawal method of birth control). Condoms made of natural materials, vaginal sponges and douches, had been used for centuries. Parish records show that there were periods, often during economic or social upheavals, when village communities had far fewer births than normal. Couples must have used birth control methods. Other cases show that unwanted children might be killed (infanticide), or else a woman might try to abort her pregnancy.

The use of birth control seems to have grown in the 1870s, particularly among the middle class. A pro-birth-control campaign attempted to swing public opinion in favour of the use of contraception, while the Bradlaugh-Besant trials of 1877–78 gave tremendous publicity to the issue. Books and pamphlets were published on contraceptive techniques. Banks (1954) argues that the middle-class support of birth control diffused down to the working class. However, many working-class couples continued to use coitus interruptus, and the abortion rate remained high. The spreading awareness of contraception was accompanied by developments in rubber technology that allowed the production of cheap and efficient contraceptives.

There were a number of individuals who were involved in the promotion of birth control in the first half of this century. The leading figure was probably Marie Stopes whose books on family planning, and her clinic work, were part of her campaign to improve the quality of family life. The Family Planning Association was formed in 1930, and by 1939 had sixty-six voluntary birth control clinics. There was, however, still resistance to the use of contraception.

The major churches were opposed to the use of birth control. The Roman Catholic Church was, and still is, implacably hostile to its use. The Church of England was also opposed to the attempts to promote the use of birth control. In 1916 a church body, the National Birth Rate Commission, expressed its outright opposition to any form of contraception other than abstinence. The Church of England gave some recognition to birth control in 1930, but did not fully accept family planning as a parental responsibility until the 1958 Lambeth Conference.

Diana Gittins (1982) argues that the attempt to encourage the use of mechanical means of birth control among the working class was part of the moral outrage against the prevalence of abortion in industrial areas. Figures examined by Gittins seem to show that only 4 per cent of the unskilled working class was using birth control before 1910. Clearly the wives in this group did not have the maximum possible number of children, which leaves open the question of how much of the fall in fertility was due to the use of abortion or abortifacients. Gittins quotes a letter to *The Times* from the family planning pioneer, Marie Stopes, in which she points out that her clinic had had 20,000 requests for abortions in three months. The final report of an Inter-Departmental Committee on Abortion in 1939 estimated that there were a daily average of 300–400 abortions. Hospital estimates suggested that between 1900 and 1936, 16 to 20 per cent of all pregnancies ended in abortion.

Evidence from the 1949 Royal Commission into contraceptive practices does show that couples had become more willing to use birth control. Of those women married between 1910 and 1919, 40 per cent used birth control, compared with 66 per cent of women married between 1935 and 1939. However, only a small proportion of the married population would have gone to clinics, read books on birth control, or consulted their doctor. Birth control remained a very private matter until the more open attitudes of the 1960s, and the development of chemical methods of contraception such as the pill.

The changing role and status of women

Demographic changes, particularly the decrease in the size of families, had a major impact on the role of women. Legal, educational, and economic changes led many politicians and writers to claim that the twentieth century had brought women near equality with men. While it must be accepted that women have made progress this century, feminist research shows that in many areas of life, including the family, women are seen to be of secondary importance to men.

There have been a number of legal changes which have improved the position of women in relation to men. The main legislation seems to have come in two periods, the first wave following the end of the First World War, and the second wave in the 1970s. The main Acts are listed below:

1918 – Votes for women aged thirty years.

1919 – Sex Disqualification (Removal) Act: women were allowed to exercise any public function, judicial office, or profession, and to serve as jurors.

1923 – Matrimonial Causes Act: this removed the sex-differentiated grounds for divorce, with infidelity becoming a ground for divorce for both sexes.

1925 – Guardianship of Infants Act: both parents now had equal rights in relation to the guardianship of their children.

1928 – Votes for women aged twenty-one and over.

1970 – Equal Pay Act: this attempted to tackle gender discrimination in employment.

1975 – Sex Discrimination Act: this was a further attempt to protect women in employment, education, etc.

1975 – Employment Protection Act: women were given legal entitlement to maternity leave.

Legal changes have opened up opportunities for women in some spheres of life, particularly employment. Changing the law may not change public attitudes, however, and private areas of life may be untouched.

Girls have also made progress on the education front, although social-class differences remain a powerful influence. The early part of this century saw the expansion of academic schooling for middle-class girls. The curriculum of these schools prepared the girl for higher education or for the job she would follow until motherhood. The secondary schooling for working-class girls, however, overemphasized the domestic skills that a girl would need in family life. This class bias in girls' education has only really weakened with the spread of the co-educational comprehensive school. Even so, girls still experience an unequal education, particularly in relation to subject choice, and in the take-up of further and higher education.

There have been major changes in work opportunities for women. At the end of the nineteenth century the biggest area of employment for women was domestic service. The two world wars gave women the opportunity to show that they could do almost any job. Since the end of the last war some traditional industries have declined. But women have benefited from the growth of jobs in the service industries. Many women are now employed in offices, local government, and the public services. Some of these jobs have given women good incomes in their own right, helping their families to a much higher standard of living. But it must be remembered that many women still occupy the lowest paid jobs in shops, factories, and hotels. Unemployment and poor job prospects hit women hard.

There has also been an increase in the number of married women working. Many young wives will work until the birth of their first child, returning to full-time work when their children are well into their schooling. The design of the modern home, the use of convenience foods, electrical gadgets, and modern fabrics make it possible to work and run the home. Many women are workers, wives, mothers, and housekeepers, all at the same time. Women are still trapped by the domestic ideology of the family.

The sociology of the post-war British family

The growth of British sociology has led to the publication of a number of studies of family life. Some of these have taken the form of community studies, looking at every aspect of life in a particular place, or else concentrating on one institution such as the family. This form of research provides us with a fascinating glimpse of social life and makes entertaining reading, but it must be remembered that these studies are snapshots in time. They are often simply a description of a community as seen through the eyes of just one or two sociologists. It is necessary to be cautious about generalizations built upon a series of community studies.

A brief review of those studies which focus on family life shows that three themes keep reappearing. First, there is the concern with kinship, particularly the shifting obligations and relationships within the family group. Second, there is an interest in changing roles within the family. Third, many of the studies explore the extent to which family form is influenced by social class.

A number of studies looked at working-class families in urban industrial settings. Dennis, Henriques, and Slaughter (1956) studied a mining community in Yorkshire. The character of the town and much of the social life was dominated by the shared experience of coal mining. The focus of the study was the dominance of the male-oriented working-class culture. The men were held together by the shared experience of working underground, shared political and trade union beliefs, and by shared leisure time in the club or pub. Husband and wife had clearly defined roles. The man brought in the wage, the wife played the role of housewife and mother.

Willmott and Young's *Family and Kinship in East London* (1957), a study of working-class family life in Bethnal Green, has gained a unique place in British sociology. It was a study of the impact of rehousing programmes on family life in east London. The research described a traditional working-class family form where the nuclear family lived close to their relatives. Husband and wife had clearly differentiated roles. The man was the main breadwinner. There was a strong relationship between the wife and her mother, a mutual exchange of services and companionship. The wife had help with her children, her marriage, and her housekeeping. In return, the mother had the support of her daughter as she reached old age.

The second part of Willmott and Young's study examined what happened to the traditional working-class family when it was rehoused on the new overspill estates on the edge of London. A better standard of housing and the relative isolation from relatives seemed to encourage the development of new shared roles.

The strong mother-daughter bond was shown in a number of other studies. Kerr's (1958) study of Ship Street looked at

60

family life in central Liverpool. Once again, the men and women seemed to live almost separate lives. Mothers and daughters had the same exchange of services as in Bethnal Green. Some of the men were away at sea, and this seemed to encourage a secondary role in the family. A similar pattern was found in Tunstall's (1962) study of the fishing community of Hull. The nature of the men's work in deep sea fishing kept them away from their families for weeks at a time. The result was a strong female family relationship.

These four studies of the urban working-class family are interesting for the way they coloured sociological attitudes to the family. They suggested a pattern of family life which was under attack from the social changes of the late 1950s and early 1960s. Housing developments emptied Bethnal Green, flattened the terraces of Hull, and dumped the Liverpool families on huge corporation estates. The large estates lacked the same community spirit. Better housing and a rising standard of living brought the nuclear family closer together. Relatives were visited by car or contacted by telephone.

The work of Elizabeth Bott (1957) provided a theoretical insight into conjugal roles. She based her ideas on in-depth interviews with twenty families. The relationship of husband and wife was shaped by the network of friends and relatives among whom they lived. This network of relationships could be strong or weak, depending on how often the couple saw friends and relatives. Bott argued that couples who had a strong closely knit network of relationships, seeing kin frequently, would have a markedly different relationship from those couples in a loosely knit network.

In a tightly knit network, the husband and wife engage in complementary but independent family roles. They have segregated conjugal roles. The wife can turn to her mother and her family for help, advice, and companionship. She runs the house and looks after the children. The man is the wage earner and gets his support from his family or his workmates. In a loosely knit network the husband and wife are more likely to have shared domestic roles and are likely to spend more of their leisure time together.

Bott suggested that the pattern of conjugal roles was linked to a number of factors. Class position was one such factor. The professional middle classes were more likely to have shared domestic roles because they moved within a loose network of friends and relations. Working-class couples were more likely to come from homogeneous and settled communities that encouraged the growth of tightly knit networks of relationships. Bott's ideas seemed to fit the evidence of the community studies and seemed to explain some of the changes affecting family life.

More evidence on family relationships came with Willmott and Young's (1960) study of the London suburb of Woodford. This revealed a home-centred family, with the couple sharing more domestic tasks. Friendship took the place of close contact with relations, but this did not mean that family ties were broken. The researchers were surprised to find the mother-daughter bond so strong in a middle-class community. Older relatives were not neglected either, for the middle-class couples kept in constant contact through the telephone or by visits in the car.

Bell's (1968) study of middle-class families in Swansea showed how families gave the financial aid that helped a young couple set themselves up as an independent family. He identified two types of family, The 'burgesses' stayed in their home area, building up their careers in local business or professions. They created a local network of contacts, partly of relatives, and partly of friends. The 'spiralists' followed a different pattern as they were both socially and physically mobile. Career moves would take the spiralists to other parts of the country, cutting them off from kin, and encouraging the growth of shared domestic roles. However, in each case, financial aid from fathers or fathers-in-law was often important in setting up home early in the marriage. This financial aid had the effect of smoothing out the income curve for the couple, giving them independence earlier than would otherwise have been possible.

Rosser and Harris (1965), in an earlier study in Swansea, pointed to a convergence of family forms. Social change had undermined the solidity of family relationships. An improved standard of living, a wider circle of marriage, and increased educational opportunities created new horizons for young couples. In particular there had been a social revolution in the status and expectations of women. Rosser and Harris suggest a convergence of family forms, a move toward shared conjugal roles and loosely knit networks of family relationships.

The symmetrical family

The many themes found in the community studies come together in Willmott and Young's *The Symmetrical Family* (1973). Demographic factors, changing patterns of kinship, changing roles and social class, are all used as part of a complete description of the development of British family life. The evidence clearly fits the 'march of progress' model, with the suggestion that the family has evolved towards a state of symmetry, a state of balance.

Willmott and Young combine survey material and historical evidence to give a rough outline of family history in Britain. They describe three stages. The stage-one family existed in pre-industrial Britain. It was a patriarchal family, dominated by the man, but with the woman playing a crucial economic role. Industrialization and the growth of large factories led to the eclipse of this family form.

The stage-two family had adapted to urban life, although Willmott and Young rather gloss over how this happened. They use historical material to illustrate the segregated roles of the working-class family. Unemployment, poverty, marital violence, and drunkenness were all threats to the stability of the family. Women had to build relationships to protect themselves and their children. The authors say that what was created was an informal women's trade union. The mother-married daughter bond was the basic means of survival for the working-class woman.

The social and demographic changes which have already been outlined helped to account for the movement towards the stage-three family. The family has grown smaller. Women have gained in status and in independence. The standard of living has improved and better housing is available to the family. The sharing of domestic roles has become more widespread. A greater proportion of married women work. The family has moved towards symmetry.

The ideal-type symmetrical family is balanced. Both husband and wife work, each contributing to the family income. Domestic roles, and the care and enjoyment of children are shared. The family tasks are eased by modern technology, from the washing machine to the electric drill.

Social changes have pushed family development towards the symmetrical form. However, Willmott and Young do not say that the stage-three family is totally dominant. All three family types could exist in society at the same time. What they do argue is that the stage-three family has diffused down from the middle class to become the common pattern among young working-class couples. They point out that there are still major social class differences in family life. Many middle-class families are still dominated by the demands of the husband's career. There is also the question of how much further the role of women can change.

Inevitably, these community studies have provided a somewhat stereotyped view of the family in post-war Britain. Family life in rural areas is often neglected. The studies by Rees (1950) of Llanfihangel, Williams (1956) of Gosforth, and Williams (1963) of Ashworthy do not readily fit the popular sociological model of family development common in sociology courses. Feminists have also questioned the description of women in these studies. Immigration has created a much wider range of family forms. The symmetrical family should not, therefore, be seen as the only model of family life in Britain. The next chapter will examine the variety of family forms that exist today.

An interesting way of studying the changes in family life is to visit any of the large country houses run by the National Trust. There are excellent guide books for most of these properties. Compare the life style of the family that owned the house with that of their domestic servants or estate workers. A visit to one of the open air industrial museums, on the other hand, may give you a chance to look at the life style of the working-class family.

Further reading

Harris (1983) gives a good account of English family life before and after the Industrial Revolution. Bell and Newby (1971) give a range of studies which can be put together to show some of the changes taking place in family life this century. Oakley (1974a) gives a very readable history of women. Rapoport, Fogarty, and Rapoport (1982) have edited one of the best collections of essays on family life today. It is almost worth reading from cover to cover, but it does run to over 500 pages!

5

Families in Britain

There is no such thing as the typical British family. The symmetrical family is not the dominant form. Rather, there is a wide range of family types existing side by side. The range of family types is partly the result of demographic factors and partly the product of changes in our social outlook, particularly our view of the role of women. There has also been the arrival of a large number of immigrants who have brought with them the family traditions of their own societies.

Households, numbers, and trends

Two sets of figures will help to explain the changing composition of British families. *Table 1* shows the changes in the composition of British households over the last twenty years. It must be remembered that the terms 'family' and 'household' have different meanings. The household is the unit that lives together in one residence. A household can be composed of just one person or many, possibly in two or more

Table 1   *Households by type in Great Britain, 1961–82*

	percentages		
	1961	*1971*	*1983*
No family			
One person – under retirement age	4	6	8
– over retirement age	7	12	16
Two or more people			
– one over retirement age	3	2	1
– all under retirement age	2	2	2
One family			
Married couple only	26	27	27
Married couple with one or two dependent children	30	26	24
Married couple with three or more dependent children	8	9	6
Married couple with independent child(ren) only	10	8	8
Lone parent with at least one dependent child	2	3	5
Lone parent with independent child (ren) only	4	4	4
Two or more families	3	1	1
Total households	100	100	100

Source: Social Trends (**15**, 1985)

families. Many nuclear families are households in their own right, but remember that the family is often wider than the household. Old age, divorce, work, and schooling can all result in the separation of the members of a nuclear family.

The second set of figures shows the distribution of households according to their size. A brief examination of *Figure 1* should make it clear that there has been a marked fall in the average size of households in Great Britain, from 3.09 people per household in 1961 to 2.64 people per household in 1983. This decline in size is the result of changes in fertility patterns, and an increase in the number and proportion of one-person households. There has been a consequent increase in the actual number of households.

There are a number of clear trends apparent in these statistics. First, the percentage of families that fit the stereotyped view of a nuclear family, i.e. a married couple and their young children, is dropping. Only 30 per cent of families in 1983 fell into this category. Two other family types are of almost equal significance in percentage terms. About 27 per cent of households are of the 'no family' type, i.e. single people or couples who live by themselves. Many of this group are elderly. Married couples make up a further 27 per cent of households. The decline in the proportion of nuclear families requires us to rethink any common-sense assumptions that we might have about what is a normal family.

The second, and perhaps the most dramatic trend is the increase in both the proportion and the number of single-person households. The proportion in this category has risen from 12 per cent in 1961 to 24 per cent in 1983. The actual number of these households has increased from under 2 million in 1961 to well over 4 million in 1981. Some of these households will be composed of young people who have set up home on their own, while others may be the single party that results from a broken marriage. But of greatest significance for society is the growing number of old people who find themselves living on their own.

A recent report by the Family Policies Studies Centre (1984) shows that we can expect to see a steady increase in the

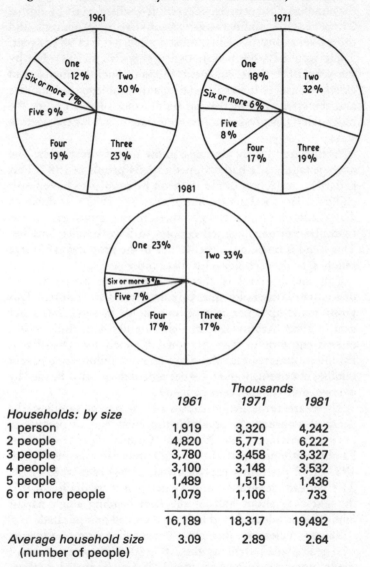

Figure 1 Households by size in Great Britain, 1961–82

	Thousands		
	1961	*1971*	*1981*
Households: by size			
1 person	1,919	3,320	4,242
2 people	4,820	5,771	6,222
3 people	3,780	3,458	3,327
4 people	3,100	3,148	3,532
5 people	1,489	1,515	1,436
6 or more people	1,079	1,106	733
	16,189	18,317	19,492
Average household size (number of people)	3.09	2.89	2.64

Source: Social Trends (**14**, 1984)

proportion of old people in society. Over the next forty years, the number of old people over sixty-five will increase by almost 21 per cent, the numbers over seventy-five by 30 per cent, and those over eighty-five will almost double, a rise of 98 per cent. There were 620,000 people over eighty-five in 1983, but by the year 2021 there will be 1,230,000. Such an increase in elderly households must create major problems for families and the state. The increasing significance of this group, the older elderly, represents a pensions time-bomb for the welfare state.

A third trend is the decrease in the size of households. The average family size had dropped to 2.64 people in 1983. This is partly a reflection of the decision by couples to have fewer children. The total period fertility rate for 1983 was down to 1.75. Economic and social pressures, together with easy access to contraception, have led couples to have smaller families. This trend is reflected in the decline in the proportion of large families, i.e. households with six or more people.

The fourth trend is the increase in the proportion of one-parent households that contain dependent children. This group made up 2 per cent of households in 1961, but 5 per cent in 1983. Around one in eight families with children is a one-parent family. The National Council for One-Parent Families estimates that there are about 1 million one-parent families in Britain, about 87.4 per cent of these being headed by women, and 12.6 per cent by men.

There are three major causes of one-parent families: the death of a parent, the breakdown of marriage, or pregnancy outside marriage. The National Council For One-Parent Families estimated that of the total number of lone mothers in 1981, 16.2 per cent were widowed, 21 per cent were single, 23.8 per cent separated, and 39 per cent were divorced. It is thought that about half of the men heading single-parent families are widowed, and half are divorced or separated.

There is a clear age difference between the women and men who head single-parent families. In 1980–81 the average age of single (unmarried) mothers was 27 years, separated mothers

34 years, divorced mothers 37 years, and widowed mothers 49 years. In contrast 86 per cent of male single parents were 35 years or over, and the average age was 45 years. What is common to both sexes is a combination of economic and emotional problems that creates many strains. These problems will be considered in the next chapter.

Marriage

Marriage continues to be of major significance. Nine out of ten people will marry. Some 90 per cent of women are married before the age of thirty. Men marry at a slightly later age, but over 90 per cent of them are married before the age of forty. However, a close examination of the statistics on marriage shows a complex and shifting pattern.

The proportion of people who can marry must depend on the sex ratio of the population. There has often been a relative shortage of men. In the nineteenth century about one-third of women of marriageable age did not marry. War, emigration, and ill health reduced the available supply of men for marriage. It is only in the last forty years that there has been a more even balance between the sexes and, in the lower age group, there are now more men than women. The number of marriages reached a peak in the early 1970s and since then has fluctuated at a lower level. The total number of marriages in England and Wales in 1982 was 342,000, the lowest figure since 1959.

The age at which marriage takes place is another variable to be considered. It will alter according to how society sees the role of young people. The young have gained in independence this century, and their economic position is relatively better than a hundred years ago. Overall, the age of marriage has declined. But the last decade has seen a slight tendency to marry later. This may reflect a desire to postpone marriage for economic, social, or educational reasons. Men still tend to be slightly older than women when they marry. In 1982 the median age at marriage for men was 25.9 years, and for women it was 23.5 years. The respective figure for 1971 was

71

24.0 and 22.0. The figures also vary according to marital status. First marriages logically take place at an earlier age than the remarriages of divorcees or widows. The median age for single women marrying in 1982 was 22.1 years, for divorced women 33.7 years, and for widows 55.4 years. The median age for single men marrying in 1982 was 24.2 years, for divorced men 36.2 years, and for widowed men 60.8 years.

It is easy to get bogged down in these demographic details of marriage. Sociologists must also ask questions about the qualitative nature of marriage, about how marriage feels to those involved. Why do we choose to marry the people we do? Why do 52 per cent of marriages still take the form of a religious ceremony? What expectations do we take into marriage, and how have these expectations changed over the years? How are these expectations related to our class, religious, or ethnic background? Above all, in what ways do men and women experience marriage differently?

Two further trends reflect a change in our approach to marriage. First, there is an increasing trend towards cohabitation, a couple living together without getting married. Cohabitation is always likely to be higher among widowed, divorced, or separate couples. But data from the General Household Survey shows that there has been a marked increase in pre-marital cohabitation. The proportion of women aged between sixteen and thirty-four years at the time of their marriage in 1978–81 who had lived with their future husbands before marriage was 21 per cent where the marriage was the first for both partners, and 67 per cent where one or both the partners were remarrying. The scale of the increase can be seen by looking at the equivalent figures for 1970–74, which were 8 per cent and 46 per cent respectively. The sociologist wants to know the reasons for this trend towards cohabitation. Is it simply a postponement of marriage, or does it represent a permanent change in the attitude to marriage?

The second trend concerns the number of remarriages that follow divorce or bereavement. In 1961 15 per cent of all marriages were remarriages. This figure had more than doubled by 1982. In 1982 64 per cent of all marriages were first marriages for both parties, while 19 per cent were first marriages for one partner only, and in a further 16 per cent of cases both partners were remarrying. The increase in the proportion of remarriages reflects the changing patterns of divorce, an issue that will be examined in the next chapter. What is clear is that remarriage reflects a continuing belief in marriage as an institution. However, a warning note needs to be sounded. Marriages where one or both of the partners have been married before are more likely to end in divorce than those of couples of the same age who are marrying for the first time.

Parenthood

Our society assumes that normal men and women will wish to be married, and that marriage will be followed by parenthood. A family without children is thought to be lacking in purpose. Women are still judged by society in terms of their maternal qualities. They are seen as gentle, caring, emotional, and protective – all qualities associated with motherhood. It is not surprising that nine out of ten married women will have children.

The average age for a woman to have her first child is about twenty-five years. This figure disguises significant variations according to social class. Working-class wives are likely to have their children at an earlier age than their middle-class counterparts. This partly reflects the increased educational and career prospects open to middle-class women. Marriage and motherhood may be postponed. Another factor that may lead young couples to delay starting a family is the economic pressure of setting up a new household.

Some married couples do not have children. For some this is a deliberate choice, a feeling that they do not want or are not suited to the rigours of parenthood. Such a choice is still seen as unusual, and perhaps unnatural. Ironically, it is often seen as a selfish act by the young couple, rather than a positive act born

73

of the belief that every child should be a wanted child. However, for a much greater number of couples, childlessness is not their choice.

It is estimated that just about 15 per cent of the adult population of childbearing age is infertile. Stanway (1980) estimates that this could affect 3 million people in Britain, producing 50,000 new cases of infertility each year. The problems that cause infertility can affect both men and women, or involve both of them. Infertility is on the increase. Stanway suggests four reasons for this: couples delaying their attempt to have their children, the impact of venereal disease on women, the prolonged use of the contraceptive pill, and the increased use of drugs and chemicals in modern life.

Infertility creates a major life crisis for some couples. Medical intervention may help, but only at the cost of an enormous intrusion into one of the most private areas of life. The failure of a couple to have children may shake a woman's view of her own femininity by denying her the status of motherhood. The man, too, may experience a profound sense of loss. The couple must face a changed future where their lives have to be rebuilt without the expectation of children.

Dual-worker families

One of the major changes that has taken place this century has been the increase in the proportion of married women working. This has risen from 21.7 per cent in 1951 to about 42.2 per cent in 1982. The result of this trend has been the expansion in the number of what have been called dual-career or dual-worker families. Sociologists have shown a particular interest in dual-worker families because they reflect the changing role relationships within the family.

There is nothing new about the phenomenon of married women working. In the pre-industrial family the wife had a key economic role, but she was not going outside the family to work. Industrialization meant that many women went to work in the factories. In 1851 24 per cent of married women worked. However, the second half of the nineteenth century saw a fall in the number of married women who worked, and by 1911 the figure had fallen to 13 per cent. The dominant ideology of the time located the role of women, particularly wives, in the home. Attitudes have changed during this century. The relative improvement in opportunities for women, together with demographic changes such as the decline in family size, have been major factors in enabling the proportion of married women working to rise to the present figure.

Gowler and Legge (1982) suggest that there are five major reasons for married women going out to work. The first reason is simple: financial need. Women go out to work for the same reason as their husbands, to bring enough money into the family to cover the basic costs of living. Many families could not survive without the extra income brought home by the wife. Other families will be able to use this income to provide the extras which mean a higher standard of living. Many of the families who featured in the sociological debate over the new affluence of the working class in the 1960s gained their affluence from the efforts of a working wife.

A second reason for a woman to go out to work is to gain more social contact, to build up a wider range of friendships than is possible as a housewife. Many wives find work rewarding simply because it brings companionship. This explanation is linked to the third reason, the need to escape the loneliness and frustration of domestic work. Gavron's (1966) study of ninety-six north London mothers suggested that many women felt that they lost their sense of freedom in marriage, particularly with the arrival of children. Work was one way to gain social contact, while also supplying extra income for the family.

Gowler and Legge also suggest that work provides the woman with a chance to develop her own personal identity outside her roles as wife and mother. The woman gains a new identity among her workmates based on her personality and her skills, rather than as the reflection of her family roles.

75

Finally, many women will return to work in order to practise a skill which they may see as important. Some women will need to train for new skills, or brush up skills learned long ago. Others will return to practise a job or profession which might have involved years of training. Teaching is one example of the kind of work to which women will return as their children grow up. Such jobs give intrinsic satisfaction, a pleasure in the work itself. They also provide a higher level of financial reward than most jobs open to married women.

Sociologists have been particularly interested in the effect that an increase in the proportion of working wives has on family life. Two themes have been highlighted in studies. First, how is the pattern of childcare affected by the decision of a wife to go out to work? Second, what impact does going out to work have on the relationship of husband and wife?

The main problem facing women who wish to return to work is the demands of dependent children. Most wives continue to work in the early years of their marriage, and it is only the arrival of children which disrupts this situation. The younger her children, or the more children there are, the more a woman is likely to be tied to the home. So long as it is women who are expected to take the major share of childcare, then it will be *their* working opportunities that are restricted.

Adequate nursery facilities would allow women to combine work with motherhood. However, these facilities are restricted. The day nurseries provided by local authorities, few as they are, are inevitably reserved for those children who are considered to be at risk, or who are in need of special care. Few employers provide nursery facilities for the children of their employees. So long as there is no shortage of labour, employers do not need to take on the extra costs of providing childcare facilities. Nursery classes attached to primary schools and voluntary playgroups provide valuable stimulation to the child, but are offering only part-time provision, perhaps for only half a day at a time. Some mothers will be able to call on relatives to look after their children while they are at work. Others will turn to childminders. The best childminders are very good, but the worst can be a danger to the children that they have in their care.

A possible answer to the childcare problem is part-time work. It may be possible for the woman to fit her working hours around the school day, but this still leaves the problem of how to cope with children during the school holidays, or when the child is sick or needs to go to the dentist. Sometimes women find themselves forced to leave their children alone for periods of the day, or else they have to give them a key to let themselves in and out of the house. Such a situation inevitably creates feelings of guilt, with the mother wondering if she is hurting the children, or worrying whether they are getting into danger or trouble.

The problems of care will be most difficult for the poorest families, where it is essential for the wife to go out to work. This group includes one-parent families. The more affluent dual-career family, where both husband and wife are in professional or commercial occupations, has a relatively easy solution to the problem of childcare. Childcare can be bought by employing a nanny, a mother's help, or even an *au pair*.

The shape of conjugal roles must also change in the dual-worker family. The woman is faced with the conflicts created by three roles – worker, housewife, and mother. The working lives of the couple could come into conflict. Whose job or career is to be given priority? Will one or both careers suffer because of the need to devote time to family matters? In many families it will be the man's work needs which are paramount, but what harm does this do the wife's career prospects?

There are also practical problems of how to run a household in which the two key adult members both work. Who is to do the shopping? When is the house going to get cleaned? Who will cook the meals? Feminist research suggests that men have still not adjusted their outlook and their roles to match the fact that they are married to working women. Oakley (1974a) suggests that although men have taken a few steps towards a more active role in housework and childcare, they still see this as women's work. Oakley (1972) wrote that the presence of men at the kitchen sink did not mean that they were becoming househusbands.

The proportion of dual-worker families is likely to increase. Their existence creates new stresses and strains for the family, but it can also bring great benefit to the individuals involved: a higher standard of living and emotional satisfaction. The extra income generated in the dual-worker family can help provide a more secure future for that family, particularly in a period of economic recession and high unemployment.

Ethnic minorities and family forms

Britain is a country with a long history of population migration. This century in particular has seen a considerable amount of both emigration and immigration. Overall, more people have left and continue to leave Britain than arrive from abroad. But people are more conscious of those who arrive than those who leave, particularly when immigration involves the arrival of groups with markedly different religious or ethnic cultures. Immigration has resulted in racial and cultural prejudice, particularly with non-white immigration from the New Commonwealth since 1945.

Immigration has brought a number of family forms to Britain that are clearly different from traditional patterns. Such families put a much greater emphasis on the demands and duties of kinship. Asian families are a clear example of this. Family members feel that they have obligations both to their kin in Britain and also to the rest of their family, who are still resident in the home village. Many Indian families in Britain continue to provide financial support for their relatives in India.

The family structure of many ethnic groups tends to be both hierarchical and patriarchal. Ballard (1982) argues that the basic pattern of the south Asian family consists of a man, his sons and grandsons, together with their wives and unmarried daughters. This family has been transferred into a British setting. The man is clearly the head of the household, controlling the family finances, and negotiating the major family decisions. R. Oakley (1982) suggests that a similar pattern is true for Greek Cypriot families living in London. The Cypriot husband is an authoritarian figure, the source of family discipline. It is the husband who handles all the external dealings of the family with the wider society. Conjugal roles are essentially segregated, although complementary to each other.

The male-dominated nature of family life creates a very different experience for women within the ethnic minorities. In the early years of immigration, many women found themselves cut off from outside society. Social and language barriers kept them trapped in the domestic setting. Some Asian families created a state of purdah for their womenfolk, setting them apart from society at large. Oakley contrasts the social isolation of Cypriot women in England with the physical openness and outdoor character of life in Cyprus.

The reason for the attempt by ethnic minorities to control the lives of women lies in the need to maintain family honour. It is important that family members do not bring shame on the family name. Every member should be seen to behave properly. Inevitably, life in a British environment has thrown up major challenges to this traditional view of family life.

Serious problems have been created with the second generation, the immigrants' children, who were born and have been brought up in the United Kingdom. School teaches these children to want more independence. The socializing influence of the family stresses loyalty and obedience. It must also be remembered that many of the first-generation immigrants grew up in societies where there was no such thing as adolescence or youth culture, so conflict is inevitable when their children act like British teenagers. However, ethnic minority families have proved to be more flexible than was at first expected. An example of this flexibility can be seen in the way that the traditional arranged marriage is being modified to allow young people some say in the process.

West Indian families in Britain present a further distinct family pattern that reflects their culture of origin. The colonial system that was based on slavery weakened the bonds between men and women. The lack of a stable employment system left the man unable to support a family by his own efforts. The mother-child relationship became the central structure of the family.

Driver (1982) and Barrow (1982) use studies of family structures in the West Indies to suggest three models of family life. The first type is the conventional nuclear family household. Such a family form was most typical of the respectable and more affluent section of the community. The second type was a common-law household, where a man and a woman lived together with their children, but without a formal marriage. Third, there was the female-dominated household, where women had to care for their children and provide an income, without the presence of a man. Studies conducted in the West Indies suggested that each type accounted for about a third of all households in the West Indies.

Driver suggests that these family forms have been transplanted into the British West Indian community. He suggests that there are two types of black family structure in Britain. There is the nuclear family, where both partners share the full range of domestic roles. But there is also the mother-centred family. Driver says this is again associated with the lack of stable employment for men. The black mother is left to bring up the children, run the home, and provide an income. She must do this in England without the range of support that she could have obtained from female relatives in the West Indies. This kind of family might even be growing in Britain, providing a clear contrast to both Asian and traditional English family patterns.

It is hard to predict how ethnic minority families will develop with the third and subsequent generations. The size of minority families is dropping rapidly. Young couples seem to be more sceptical about the need to maintain such a wide family network. But the young Asians, Chinese, and Cypriots are well aware of their different cultural heritages. For many of these young people, their family life will be a compromise between the two cultures they inhabit.

Activity

The statistics in a book like this soon date. One way for you to obtain the latest statistics, and at the same time improve your sociological knowledge of the family, is for you to learn your way round the latest edition of *Social Trends*. Look up the most recent figures on births, marriages, divorces, and deaths. Do they still fit the trends outlined in this book? If you want more detailed figures, for instance quarterly, or broken down by geographical region, then write for the latest OPCS monitors. They can be obtained from the Office of Population Censuses and Surveys, St Catherine's House, 10 Kingsway, London WC2B 6JP.

Further reading

Once again it is worth consulting the articles in Rapoport, Fogarty, and Rapoport (1982). Delamont (1980) has a good chapter on how women experience parenthood. Kitzinger (1978), although not a sociologist, gives a stimulating view of motherhood. Khan (1979) has edited a useful collection of contributions on the strains experienced by ethnic minority families in Britain.

6

Is the family in crisis?

Sociologists who support the 'march of progress' model see the modern family as well adapted to the needs and pressures of modern industrial society. Fletcher (1966) argues that there has been a general improvement in public life which has strengthened the family. He points to improvements in the relationship between husband and wife, between parents and children, and between the family and the state. Other sociologists argue that the family has not made progress, and now faces a major crisis.

Politicians in the United States, in Britain, and in many other countries have pointed to the dangers that could occur if there is a weakened or an unstable family structure. The annual publication of divorce statistics creates a moral panic in the media on the health of the family. Social problems such as juvenile crime or drug-taking are blamed on a disintegrating family life. Instead of being seen as a 'good fit', the modern family is seen to be in crisis.

The sociological value of this crisis model can be examined

by looking at four themes: the rising divorce rate, the amount of violence in the family, the situation of one-parent families, and the position of the elderly in society.

The breakdown of marriage

The rising divorce rate

Divorce marks the legal termination of a marriage relationship. A marriage can also be ended by annulment, or through the couple separating. It must also be remembered that an unhappy marriage need not end in divorce. Many unhappy couples will stay together, perhaps for religious reasons, perhaps because of the children.

In Britain, as in most industrial societies, there has been a steady rise in the divorce rate. Newspaper headlines claim that one in three marriages now ends in divorce, a figure that is said to herald the demise of the family. Sociologists take a more restrained view of the increase in divorce, but must still admit that the divorce graph shows a dramatic increase. *Figure 2* shows that a few hundred divorces per annum at the start of the century have now become nearly 150,000 a year.

A number of explanations can be put forward to account for this increase. Legal changes are very important. It was not easy to obtain a divorce before the middle of last century. A divorce was only granted by obtaining a Private Act of Parliament; the expense and effort involved meant that it remained the privilege of the rich. A law in 1857 made divorce easier, and a special Divorce Court was set up. Divorce remained too expensive for ordinary people, however, and the annual average number of divorces was still less than 150.

Women could not obtain a divorce on equal terms with men. Not only had women to prove that their husbands were guilty of adultery, they had to prove that they had committed a matrimonial offence such as cruelty or rape. This legal double standard was not altered until 1923, and even then

Figure 2 Divorce decrees absolute in England and Wales, 1901–82

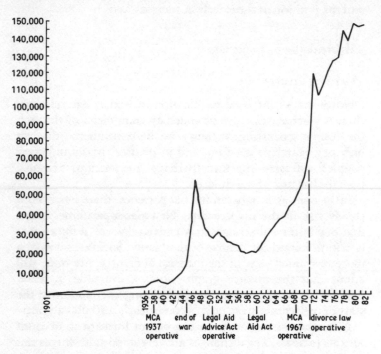

women had the problem of raising enough money to take a divorce case to court.

The 1937 Matrimonial Causes Act extended the grounds of divorce beyond adultery to include insanity, desertion, and cruelty. It was this Act that laid the legal framework of divorce law for the next thirty years. The law had become relatively straightforward; it was finance that stopped many people going to court to end their marriages.

The Second World War disrupted a large number of marriages. Separation strained many relationships, while others came to regret a hasty marriage. It was not surprising that, by the end of the war, there was a backlog of broken

84

marriages waiting to go to court. The immediate post-war years saw a record level of divorce, but once the backlog was cleared, the divorce rate fell. It was not until the 1960s that the divorce rate began to rise steadily.

The most dramatic change in the level of divorce results from the bill to reform the divorce law which was presented to parliament in 1969, coming into force in 1971. There was now only one ground on which a divorce petition could be based, the irretrievable breakdown of marriage. Those wanting a divorce had to prove that the marriage had broken down by showing that the partners had lived apart, that they had been deserted, or that they could not accept their partner's adultery or cruelty. What was significant about the new legislation was that it allowed divorce by 'consent'. A couple who had lived apart for two years and who both wanted a divorce could obtain one. Even where one partner did not want a divorce, perhaps for religious reasons, the other partner could petition for a divorce after five years' separation. Couples did not even have to go to court, they could divorce by post.

The change in the law had an immediate impact on the divorce figures. The first full year to which the new law applied was 1972, and in that year there were over 119,000 divorces made absolute in England and Wales. The courts were once again dealing with a backlog of broken marriages. However, after a small drop in the figures in 1973–74, the divorce rate has continued to rise, and now over 145,000 divorces are granted every year.

It is necessary to examine the other reasons that have been used to explain the rise in divorce. The first of these is the economic factor. Couples can now afford divorce more easily than at any time in the past. A straightforward 'do-it-yourself' divorce on the grounds of separation with consent costs less than £50. It is the complicated and bitter wrangles over children and property which produce the large legal bills. Those with low incomes can use the Legal Aid Scheme to cover most of their costs.

The financial consequences of a divorce are also more easily affordable. The rise in incomes and the increased opportunities for married or divorced women to go out to work do enable both parties to a divorce to make a living. The growth in home ownership means that there may be a profit on the sale of the house that can be shared by the partners. The partners may then have to move to smaller accommodation, or perhaps approach the local authority for help with council housing. The social security system will help maintain the income of those unable to go back to work straight away, for example a young mother. Having said that divorce is now affordable, it must also be said that divorce must involve an economic loss, and for many families it is an economic disaster. One-parent families created by divorce often slide into poverty. The break-up of a family shows more clearly than anything else the economic function of the family.

The other major reason for an increase in the divorce rate is concerned with our changing attitude to marriage. The traditional Christian approach to marriage has been, and to some extent still is, opposed to divorce. Secularization has weakened our attachment to the religious view of marriage as being a union for life. There are now almost equal numbers of civil marriages in registry offices as there are religious marriages in churches or other religious buildings. The result is that the break-up of a marriage is seen less as a moral crisis and more as a matter of personal happiness. Much of the stigma has now gone from divorce.

Marriage is now viewed as part of the individual's search for happiness. The ideal marriage is seen to be a balance of romantic love and good practical housekeeping. The break-down of the marriage is to be seen as a loss of happiness, and the decision to divorce is taken in the light of what is best for the couple and any children. Perhaps sociologists have asked the wrong questions. Rather than concentrating on why there are divorces, sociologists could spend more time looking at marriage. The important question may well be why do we marry the people we do, and why do we stay married to them?

Who divorces?

Sociologists have clear evidence about some of the factors which contribute to the breakdown of a marriage. A marriage between two people from very different backgrounds is more at risk. Such a relationship may be under extra pressure from relatives or friends who may not approve of cutting across class, religious, or ethnic boundaries. The divorce rate is higher in urban than rural areas, possibly because couples marrying in the country are more likely to come from similar backgrounds. Marriages after a very short acquaintance are also risky. But the most crucial factor could be age.

This century has seen a trend towards earlier marriage, particularly for the working class. Long engagements, often lasting several years, are a thing of the past. The young couple of today may have the money to marry before they have the psychological maturity to sustain the relationship. One in two teenage brides, and six out of ten teenage bridegrooms can expect their marriages to end in divorce.

Young brides may be pregnant at marriage, putting an extra strain on the relationship. However, there is a decline in these 'shotgun' marriages. In 1971 more than one in three of the 186,000 babies conceived outside marriage were subsequently legitimized by marriage, the rest being born illegitimate or aborted. By 1981 only 19 per cent of these extra-marital conceptions were followed by marriage. This seems to reflect a change in our attitude to the single parent and the couple who cohabit. Roughly one-quarter of all couples who marry have lived together. At the same time, more efficient contraception and the availability of abortion have reduced the number of brides under the age of twenty who are pregnant.

In 1982 there were 147,000 divorces in England and Wales, twelve divorces for every 1,000 couples. Roughly one in three marriages will now end in divorce. In 1982, 42,000 of the couples divorcing had no children. Some of these marriages would be ending before any children were born; in others, childlessness might be a major factor. Nevertheless, the families involved in divorce contained over 158,000 children under the age of sixteen.

The rise in the divorce rate does not mean that people have lost faith in marriage as an institution. The experience of an unhappy marriage does not prevent couples trying again. In 1982 about 64 per cent of all marriages were first marriages for both partners. In 19 per cent of marriages one partner was remarrying and in 16 per cent both partners were remarrying. Unfortunately, the divorcee who marries again is almost twice as likely to get divorced again!

Divorce may have lost much of its social stigma but it still causes a tremendous amount of individual unhappiness. Children must live through the hurt created by divorce, and may suffer financial and emotional problems as part of a one-parent family. Couples may fight over the financial settlement. Divorced wives have the particular problem of getting maintenance orders enforced. This is important, given that 70 per cent of divorce proceedings are started by wives.

New legislation on divorce came into force at the end of 1984. There are two elements to the new legislation. First, it reduces from three years to one year the period before a married couple can petition for a divorce. This has met opposition from those who see it as one further step in the weakening of marriage as an institution. But the second and even more controversial element of the new law concerns financial settlements. The 'conduct' of the partners now becomes an element in any court decision on a financial settlement. This has been seen by some groups as part of a 'male backlash', an attempt to end settlements which are said to give some women 'a meal ticket for life'. It is too early to say what effect this will have on maintenance awards, particularly as the needs of dependent children must still be put first. But it will do nothing to reduce the personal suffering of a divorce, particularly if individual conduct is once again to become the subject of moral scrutiny.

Violence in the family

Violence is one of the main dysfunctional aspects of family life. Many murders and a high proportion of physical assaults take place within the family. Family violence is largely directed against wives and children.

Battered wives

The sociologist looking at the violence directed at wives needs to ask three questions. How much violence is there in marriage? What causes this violence? Why do physically abused wives stay in violent marriages? It is not easy to find the answers to these questions as so much violence is hidden. Women who have been abused experience fear, shame, and a sense of degradation. The public admission of the violence present in their marriage would make them feel a strong sense of failure.

Estimates on the extent of violence in the family vary widely and depend on whether you include the 'milder' cases of slapping, pushing, and grabbing. Marsden and Owens (1975) suggest that perhaps one in a hundred marriages in the United Kingdom is violent, a total of some 140,000 marriages. Gettes (1979) argues that in the United States, four out of a hundred women are the victims of severe physical violence in marriage each year, a total of 2 million women. It is not just how many wives are assaulted that is important, it is how often they are assaulted. Dobash and Dobash (1980) estimated that the 109 battered wives they interviewed in Scotland had experienced 32,000 assaults.

The study by the Dobashes seems to suggest that sexual jealousy is a major trigger to violent behaviour. Money troubles, arguments over meals or the house, and drink are often involved. Other research suggests that perhaps half of the battering husbands and a quarter of the wives had come from homes where there had been violence. Their reaction to stress would often take a violent form. Some women knowingly married a violent man, hoping to reform him through marriage.

The experience and example of violence as a child may give a wife such a negative self-image that she comes to accept a subordinate place in marriage. But many battered wives come from a normal, non-violent family background and might be expected to leave a violent husband. Fear and the threat of economic hardship if she leaves keep her with her husband. But many other wives continue to hope that their husbands will change and that the battering will stop.

Battered wives have not always had the support from family, friends, or the welfare services when they most needed help. Friends may not believe their accounts or may somehow think that they were at fault. Many marriages have a 'Jekyll and Hyde' quality which disguises the violence with a veneer of normality. Wives may not want to go to the police for help and, in any case, the police are relatively ineffective unless the wife is willing to take legal proceedings against her husband.

There has been a growth in voluntary support for the battered wife. Much of this has been self-help within the women's movement. Britain now has several hundred refuges where women can escape from a violent marriage. The women's movement works in another area of violent behaviour, sexual assault. Rape Crisis centres, although mainly dealing with sexual assaults outside the family, do help with sexual assault within a marriage. The issue of rape within marriage, and also the other major area of sexual violence, incest, raise uncomfortable questions about the family. Feminists are probably right to argue that such issues can only be resolved when there is a more equal power relationship within the family.

Child abuse

Physical, sexual, and psychological violence directed against children is the second 'dark' area of family life. Once again it is a difficult area to investigate. No parent wants to admit that they have mistreated their child. What is mistreatment? Society gives parents the right to control their own children but fails to write the rules to govern the relationship. Even the best parents find themselves having to hold back strong feelings of anger and frustration at their children, and sometimes fear that they will lose control.

In order to appear in the statistics on child abuse, cases need to be identified as such by doctors, hospital staff, or social workers. Some children may be spotted by health visitors, social workers, or teachers as being at risk. Such children may be put on the 'at risk' register or placed under a care order. But there is always the chance that children at risk may slip through the net and appear as another tragic victim of family violence. The press are quick to give publicity to any case which shows that the social services or health authority have failed to protect or help a young child.

The most recent evidence on the scale and causes of violence against children comes from the National Society for the Prevention of Cruelty to Children (Creighton 1984). The evidence for this study was taken from the 6,532 notified cases of child abuse, or serious risk of abuse, which were reported by the NSPCC Special Units in the period 1977 to 1982. The NSPCC register cases of abuse under four criteria. These are physical injury, physical neglect, failure to thrive and emotional abuse, and living in the same household as a person previously involved in child abuse.

Table 2 shows the estimates of the national incidence of physical abuse based on an NSPCC sample that covers 10 per cent of the child population of England and Wales.

These statistics are broken down in Creighton's study by a number of criteria, including the age of the child, the sex of the child, the social class background of parents, birth weight, parental situation, family size, accommodation, stress factors, and sources of referral. This has enabled the NSPCC to make a good assessment of the scale and nature of child abuse.

Table 2 *Estimates of national incidence of physical abuse by year*

	1977	1978	1979	1980	1981	1982
estimated number of children 0–14 physically abused in England and Wales	4,699	4,803	4,493	5,152	5,723	6,388
severity breakdowns fatal and seriously injured	822	749	553	606	646	647
moderately injured	3,877	4,054	3,940	4,546	5,077	5,741

Source: Creighton (1984)

The first broad conclusion is that the majority of the physically injured children were moderately rather than seriously injured. There has been a lot of debate over the number of child deaths per year. The NSPCC have used their figures to give estimates of child deaths ranging from forty-four to seventy-four over the period 1977 to 1982. The majority of children who died in suspicious circumstances appear to have died as a result of a single assault on them. A study of newspaper reports also shows a number of cases each year of family murders, often followed by the suicide of the remaining adult.

The majority of children received soft tissue injuries only, i.e. bruises, welts, cuts, and burns. *Table 2* shows that there is a downward trend in the percentage of fatal and serious injuries, from 16.8 per cent of physically injured children in 1977 to 10.1 per cent in 1982. However, there has been an increase in the number of moderately injured. *Table 3* gives an indication of the frequency of physical injury.

Table 3   *Physically injured rate*

	1977	1980	1982
physically injured per 1,000 under 15s	0.43	0.50	0.63
physically injured per 1,000 under 5s	0.92	1.03	1.20

Source: Creighton (1984)

The second set of findings concerns the children most likely to be injured. The youngest age groups, boys, low birth weight children, and illegitimate children were all over-represented among those children injured. The child under a year old is most vulnerable. Injury and neglect are bound to have a major impact at this age. Children deprived of the right physical and emotional environment will not thrive. Gender is also a key variable. Boys outnumber girls in most cases of abuse. It is only in sexual abuse cases that girls are in a majority, where they are four times more likely to be the victim than boys.

The third set of findings concerns the social characteristics of the family, and the effect that the family environment has on the child. There was an over-representation of parents from semi-skilled and unskilled occupations, the lowest socio-economic groups. Unemployment rates were rising in the period of the study and can be expected to have hit this group hardest. The parents involved were clearly distinguished from others with this background by their early entry into parenthood, their marital instability, and their larger-than-average families. Nearly half the fathers had criminal records, often involving a disturbing amount of violence. These families proved to be less settled than the average, and had moved home more frequently.

It is clear that these are families under great stress. The causes of the stress are very complex. The NSPCC report says that the most frequently quoted stress factors were marital discord, unemployment of the main breadwinner, and financial problems. These may be associated with a fourth factor, poor parental self-esteem.

A sociological approach to these findings raises a number of issues. To what extent is child abuse associated with social class? This must involve us in a debate over the meaning of the statistics. The sociological criticism of the nature of statistics has been well illustrated in fields such as the study of deviance, or the sociology of health. Figures on child abuse are also socially constructed. They may underestimate the scale of violence among middle-class families. Each case depends on some expert, for instance a doctor in a casualty department, labelling a particular child as a victim of abuse. Such sociological caution about the nature of these statistics should not be seen to detract from the significance of this NSPCC report. Violence against children is a major social problem. The solution to the problem is seen by the community to be intervention by social work agencies. Sociologists are interested in these points of intervention by the state, because they reflect the current ideology of the family. This theme will be taken up in the final chapter.

One-parent families

The third major area of concern over the health of the family looks at the one-parent family. One in eight families in Britain is a one-parent family. There is public concern because of an apparently rapid increase in this form of family. Between 1971 and 1981 the number of lone parents increased by over 70 per cent, and the number of children in one-parent families by 62 per cent, from 1 million to 1.6 million. The involvement of so many children makes this type of family an important social policy issue.

The one-parent family is often viewed as a pathological form, an unfortunate and deviant structure which reflects both individual and communal failure. This viewpoint has led to a

94

concentration on two issues in particular, the illegitimate birth and the family broken by divorce. However as Jackson (1982) points out, there are several different types of one-parent family. Nor should they always be seen as failures. The formation of a one-parent family can be a very positive step, often marking the move away from unhappy or harmful relationships.

Bereavement, divorce, cohabitation, and births outside marriage are all key factors in the creation of one-parent families. Such families are often a temporary stage between the break-up of one family and the formation of another by remarriage. This movement in and out of one-parent families means that far more people have experienced this situation than the figures suggest. Popay (1983) estimates that over 12 per cent of all children have at one time lived in a one-parent family.

In the years 1979–81 some 11.9 per cent of families in Britain with children were one-parent families. Of these, 87.4 per cent were headed by a woman and 12.6 per cent by men. Jackson (1982) points out some of the issues involved. The traditional socialization of girls means that in some ways women are better at handling the practical problems of childcare and housework. They may also develop an extremely close emotional bond with their children, a relationship that may come to dominate their social life. But women are clearly at an economic disadvantage in a society where the state assumes a man will head the family as breadwinner. Our economic life limits the possibilities of a lone mother earning a good income while continuing to look after her children. There are, of course, exceptions. The single parent with a professional career may be able to afford to buy in help, for example a nanny.

More attention is now being paid to the situation of one-parent families which are headed by a man. Out of 975,000 one-parent families in Great Britain in 1981, approximately 110,000 were headed by men. It is thought that about half of these families were the result of the death of the wife, and half were the result of marital failure. The number of widowers in this group raised the average age of these male single parents to forty-five years, considerably higher than the figure for women. These fathers looked after about 185,000 children, 95 per cent of whom were of school age.

Fathers face particular problems as single parents. Our society expects men to work, and does not expect them to have their working life disrupted by the need to care for a sick child, or a visit to the dentist. Some men may be able to afford to pay for help in the home or with the children, but many will not. Some men have the experience or skills to look after young children or do the housework, but many do not, although they can learn. However, there may be opposition to them taking on this family role, particularly if their children are very young or are of the opposite sex. Some men will have to fight for their right to look after their children, rather than see them go into care or to a relative. Single parenthood for a man may have to be a deliberate and positive choice.

Births to single women

Slightly more than 14 per cent of all babies born in England and Wales in 1982 were to single, widowed, separated, or divorced women. There were 89,857 such births to single women in 1982. It should not be assumed that these births were only to one-parent families. Many of the births will have been to cohabiting couples who may or may not have married at a later stage. A further 40,772 children born in 1982 were conceived outside marriage, but were legitimized by the marriage of their parents before the birth of the child.

The greatest social concern is with the young unmarried mother. In 1982 there were 27,578 live births to women under the age of nineteen years, nearly 31 per cent of all births to single women; 1,161 of these births were to girls under sixteen years of age, the so-called schoolgirl mothers. The children of young mothers are often considered to be at risk. The perinatal and infant mortality rates are significantly higher for these children. The young mother will face great hardship unless she can get support from the father or her own family. There is still a stigma attached to an illegitimate birth, even though it is much reduced compared with the beginning of the century. It is no surprise that so many young women prefer to have an abortion. The sixteen to nineteen age group has the highest rate of abortion, 19.25 per 1,000 women.

Sociologists and social historians have taken an interest in illegitimacy, seeing in it a reflection of the current attitudes to the morality of family life. Peter Laslett (1977) has shown that illegitimacy in England has an extremely complicated history, rising and falling according to the economic and social influences of the day. Illegitimate births were common enough in pre-industrial England, and such births did not always earn social disapproval. There was a big increase in illegitimate births at the start of the nineteenth century, followed by an apparent fall in the Victorian period.

Edwin Shorter (1976) argues that there have been two sexual revolutions in Europe, the first in the late eighteenth century and the second taking place now, in the latter part of the twentieth century. The growth in the influence of the adolescent peer group, the increased emphasis in society on sexuality, and the instability of marriage are all factors which help explain a change in sexual behaviour. Contraception and abortion have reduced illegitimate births among older unmarried women. But the teenage rate has continued to climb, and has risen as a proportion of total births at a time when the total period fertility rate has fallen.

Society has softened its attitude towards the unmarried mother. Families are now more sympathetic. Shotgun marriages are less common, and there has been a dramatic fall in the number of babies placed for adoption. The young mother is more likely to keep her child than a decade ago, but the single parent will still face great economic problems. One-parent families make up almost half of families with children on supplementary benefit, and are much less likely to have the normal range of consumer goods. Successive governments

97

have all failed to tackle this problem of the low standard of living of the young mother and, given the current economic climate, there is little reason to believe that this will change.

Caring for the elderly

The previous chapter pointed out that the ageing of the population is proving to be a particular problem for planning and policy purposes. This century has seen the number of people aged over sixty-five rise from just over 1.5 million to over 8 million, from 5 per cent of the population to 15 per cent. The majority of the elderly in the lower half of the age group continue to lead healthy and active lives. The major concern is with the older elderly. In 1901 there were only 57,000 people over eighty-five years of age. By 1983 the figure had risen to 620,000, and by 2021 population projections suggest a figure of 1,230,000. The older elderly present the social services and the family with a major problem of care.

Many of the elderly will try to live an independent life, maintaining their own home and looking after their own needs. The majority of old people are not isolated. The 1980 General Household Survey found that 32 per cent of elderly people over sixty-five saw a relative or friend every day or nearly every day. Another 29 per cent saw one two or three times a week. It is the remaining group who give cause for concern.

Social services departments provide a wide range of services to help the elderly in their own homes. Most people want to stay in familiar surroundings. It is also very much cheaper to support old people in their own homes than to put them into residential care. Local authorities provide home helps, day centres, luncheon clubs, and other social centres for the elderly. The community nursing services try to maintain the individual's health to a standard which will enable them to continue to live an independent life.

The crisis comes when old people become too frail to continue to care for themselves. One possibility is for the old person to enter a residential home, but places in local authority homes are often scarce, and may have waiting lists. Private homes can cost well over £150 a week, beyond the resources of many families. Only about 5 per cent of the over sixty-fives are in institutional care.

Further problems are created by the physiological weaknesses of old age such as the lack of mobility, the deterioration of the senses, and the onset of psycho-geriatric problems. Health authorities have had to increase the number of long-stay beds for psycho-geriatric patients. All these services cost a great deal of money. The government is trying to reduce the spending of local authorities and, in many areas, financial cuts have brought health and social services to crisis point. The family with elderly members must cope with the problem as best it can.

The family has always looked after its elderly members, even though the media often give the impression that old people are neglected by their relatives. Economic pressure on the local authorities means that the family must continue to carry this responsibility. A report from the Family Policy Studies Centre (1984) points out that there are 1.25 million carers in Britain, the majority looking after elderly relatives. Three-quarters of these carers are women. Estimates suggest that half of all housewives aged thirty-five to sixty-four can expect at some time to have to look after an elderly or infirm person, normally a relative.

The caring role puts great strain on the family. Time, effort, space, and expense are all diverted away from other family activities. Although caring is often a loving and positive experience, it can also be a very destructive one. This is particularly true for the woman who acts as the sole carer, giving up a large part of her life to look after a relative. She may sacrifice her chance of marriage, her career opportunities, and the best years of her life. The economic saving to the state is considerable, but at what personal cost?

It is clear that it is a myth to say that the modern family neglects old people. We tend to forget that, in the last century, old people often faced the rigours of the workhouse because their families were unable to support them. The FPSC report says that the carers in the family are the 'forgotten army' of the welfare state. They argue that government policy must be changed to support the family in caring for old people.

A concluding note

Fletcher (1966) argued that the modern nuclear family is well adapted to the demands of modern society. The evidence of this chapter suggests that this was perhaps an over-optimistic view. The family faces many problems that can cause much personal misery.

Sociology has not, and is not, capable of coming to a general conclusion on whether the modern family is a success or a failure. Some studies have said that the family is in decline, others have said it is not. Some sociologists have said it would be good for both the individual and society if the family did decline, others say that would be a disaster. What is clear is that sociological studies show a wide range of family types that seem to be able to survive a wide range of pressures.

Further reading

The last two chapters of Harris (1983) discuss a wide range of the issues involved in the debate over the health of the family. Rapoport, Fogarty, and Rapoport (1982) provide good accounts of each of the issues discussed in the chapter. Pizzey (1974) provides a graphic account of violence in the family, and of the attempts to provide support for battered wives. A. Oakley (1982) touches on all of the themes in her aptly titled study Subject Women.

Some of the most interesting material comes from the specialist interest groups working in the social policy field. The addresses of three of these groups are printed below. Each publishes research pamphlets, newsletters, or policy statements. A stamped addressed envelope will bring their publications list. It should be remembered that each of these groups is a charity, and therefore they are not able to provide huge amounts of free, glossy material. However, they are always ready to provide material which is good value for money, and is always relevant and bang up to date.

The Family Policy Studies Centre (formerly the Study Commission on the Family)
3 Park Road
London NW1 6XN

One-Parent Families (The National Council for One-Parent Families)
255 Kentish Town Road
London NW5 2LX

The National Society for the Prevention of Cruelty to Children (NSPCC)
67 Saffron Hill
London EC1N 8RS

7

The family, the state, and the future

This final chapter is an attempt to look at the possibilities of change for the family. At various times, individuals or groups have tried to move the family in a specific direction of development. Such attempts have had a limited success. Any attempt to change the family has to come to terms with how the state views the role of the family. The family exists within the framework of institutions and power groups that control the political life of society. The state has policies which help shape the family system. This does not stop the family from changing or evolving into new forms. It is at least possible to identify some of the forces that may in the future shape the development of the family.

The search for an alternative family

One of the most notable efforts at creating an alternative family was the kibbutzim movement of Israel. The kibbutz is an attempt to create a community which is a fusion of socialist and Zionist beliefs. Jewish settlers arriving in Palestine early this century set up communities which would be self-supporting, and which would allow the expression of socialist ideals. These communities were well suited to the harsh physical conditions and the hostile political environment. Kibbutzniks accepted an austere life in order to build the foundations of their Jewish home state. The members of the kibbutzim played a key role in the subsequent creation and development of the state of Israel.

A kibbutz is designed to be a democratic community. A meeting of members controls the policy of the community. The members are served by a secretariat, and by a series of committees. The means of production are owned by the whole community. The economic and social life of the kibbutz is planned by the committees. Adults work at a range of tasks, some of which are rotated to provide variety. The kibbutz sets a target standard of living through its budget which meets the clothing, housing, and food needs of its members. Adults are not paid a wage, but share the standard of life provided by the community.

In the early days of some kibbutzim there was an attempt to downgrade the importance of the family. The main means of achieving this was through a unique system of collective education. The link between parents and children was played down. Infant children were brought up in the children's house by a *metapelet*. The *metapelet* was nurse, housemother, and educator. She was charged with handling the delicate educational and psychological problems of child development. Kibbutz education put the emphasis on community identity, rather than on the development of individual self. The role of the parents in bringing up children was to be limited. They had contact with, and showed their child love, but the key decisions on the future of that child lay with the community.

The anti-family stage of the kibbutz movement soon passed, and the relationship between the individual family and the community has clearly altered. Irvine (1980) has traced some of the changes that have taken place with regard to the role of

103

parents. Western theories of child development have led to a stronger emphasis on the role of parents in the first two or three years of a child's life. Parents no longer limit themselves to a 'daily visit', and the result has been a strengthening of the parent-child relationship. The kibbutzniks who care for the children are now more likely to involve parents in their task.

The whole social life of the kibbutz has now begun to change. There is more emphasis on the family as a unit. As the standard of living within the kibbutzim has risen, the communities have been able to give more priority to the housing needs and living conditions of married couples. This has encouraged the growth of familistic tendencies, even to the extent in some kibbutzim of the introduction of separate sleeping arrangements for parents and their children. The ideology of the kibbutz must change to accommodate these arrangements, with the changes being seen as a way to free the family to concentrate on its most important functions.

Sociologists have shown great interest in the ways that the kibbutz has adjusted to modern conditions. Present-day Israel is vastly different from the Palestine that existed at the start of this century. The development of a western-style economy, based on an urban life style, has weakened the mystique of the kibbutz. Young people have been exposed to the influences of this wider society, to the mass media, and to the experience of travel. The kibbutz has had to accommodate these changes. What has interested sociologists and psychologists is the way in which the kibbutz movement has taken the return of the family into its structure. These changes have raised problems for women. Are they to be forced back into traditional roles? If so, does this mark the end of the kibbutzim as a radical alternative to traditional family forms?

A second major attempt to find an alternative family structure came with the growth of the commune movement in the 1960s. The ideal of communal living is not new. Groups like the Diggers in seventeenth-century England or Oneida in nineteenth-century America show how people searched for a communal solution to their problems. The liberal and critical atmosphere of the 1960s suggested to some individuals that communal living might provide one way to shed the constraints of modern society. The conventional nuclear family was seen as one of the institutions that did most to repress the individual. The commune movement was an attempt to face the critical issues raised by radical psychiatrists such as Laing and Cooper.

Communes are a form of alternative household. They are formed by groups of adults, with or without children, who consciously try to live in a communal household which attempts to restructure normal domestic and kin relations. McCulloch (1982), in one of his most recent articles on communes, suggests that there is a wide range of possible household forms. At one end are attempts by couples to live in an 'open marriage', while at the other end are the full-blown attempts at communal households. He develops the typology suggested by Lee (1979) as a means of analysis of communal households. Lee suggested two major types of experimental household, the 'communal' and the 'collective'. In the communal household, each individual adult tries to develop a shared life with all the other adults. On the other hand, in the collective household, the basic unit remains the nuclear family. Each nuclear family shares resources with other families.

Researchers have identified a number of reasons for the creation of communes. Many of the long-lasting communes are based on strongly held religious or political beliefs. The believers wish to put their faith or their ideology into practice in every part of their life. Communal living is one way of doing this. Others saw communal living as an economical way to live, a way to practise self-sufficiency, or as a way to live off artistic talents. Some communes had a therapeutic basis, and tried to create an environment that supported those suffering from some personal or psychiatric problem. However, many of the new wave of communes seem to have been set up for psycho-social reasons, as a means to help self-discovery and to release the creative elements within the individual.

What seems to be common to many of these alternative households is the attempt to create an intimate group bound together by strong relationships, but at the same time allowing open and non-exclusive relationships. The ideal commune would create strong, caring, and loving relationships, while leaving the individual free from over-possessive attachments. Sadly, many communes failed to live up to these ideal standards and split up. Rigby (1974) estimated that there were one hundred communes in Britain. McCulloch suggests that there are now no more than fifty.

There are a number of key problems which communes have not found easy to solve. Many communes have had a financial struggle to survive. It is not easy to set up a self-sufficient group in England. Groups have to rely on the capital brought in by members, or on what can be earned through regular work. Money problems create tensions that may result in power struggles. It may also create two kinds of commune member, the member of the inner core, and the fringe member. Such a division opens up areas of potential conflict over the allocation of resources within the household.

Communes are also faced with the problem of caring for children. The ideals of the commune may suggest that all adults will help to care for all children. The reality is often that women continue to bear the burden of childcare, denying them equal opportunities for self-development. Indeed, the young mother who is not attached to a man provides the commune with a major emotional and practical challenge.

There is also a generation problem in communes. At what age do children become accepted as adult members of the commune? Is the commune a better environment for handling the problems of adolescence? At what age does a young person become a sexual participant in the life of the commune? How does a commune deal with the elderly? Are they going to be welcome in the alternative household? No easy solution exists for these problems.

It is clear that neither kibbutzim nor communes have found it easy to establish an alternative to conventional family life. However, they do represent very real attempts to grapple with some of the major dysfunctions of modern family life. They are unlikely to be the last attempts to create alternative family structures.

The view from the state

It is clear that the family is of great significance to the state. Governments and political parties in every society have to develop policies and pass legislation which affects the family. The social welfare systems of most developed countries place great importance on the role of the family and, in developing countries, the family is just as significant an institution. Changes in family patterns are therefore of great significance to the state.

Most government action is claimed to be in support of the family. The legislation passed in the nineteenth century to control the working lives of women and children was seen as part of the attempt to improve the social conditions of the working-class family. Feminists would also say that it reflected a particular ideological view which saw the place of women as being in the home. The development of the twentieth-century welfare state is seen as giving support to the family. The Beveridge Report of 1942 advocated welfare services which would remove the evils of 'Want, Disease, Squalor, Ignorance, and Idleness'. The expected result was a healthier, happier family and a stronger nation.

There are a number of examples of state attempts to change the nature of family life. One notable example was the campaign by the post-revolutionary Soviet government to destroy the pre-revolutionary form of the family. The Russian government saw the traditional family as an obstacle to the growth of a truly socialist society. It was therefore seen to be necessary to change the family. Legislation made divorce and abortion easy to obtain. New laws guaranteed women equal status with men. The government encouraged the development of communal facilities for the care of children. Education stressed communal rather than family loyalties. This all fitted the government's expectation that the family would wither away, to be replaced by broader community institutions.

These government measures failed to destroy the family. More damage was probably done by the severe economic crises that hit the Soviet Union in the 1920s. Civil war, the collectivization of agriculture, famine, political purges, and urbanization all created problems for family life. One result was a rapid falling off in the birth rate.

The Soviet government changed the direction of its family policies in the 1930s, and started to strengthen family life. Abortion was made illegal in 1936. Marriage and divorce laws were tightened. Families were encouraged to have more children, and the family allowance system was weighted towards larger families. The media glorified motherhood and fatherhood. Even today, the state gives great support to the family. Communal nurseries help families combine work and childrearing. The emphasis on the community's role in working with the family still distinguishes the Soviet family from its west European counterpart.

Many other governments have shown concern over fluctuations in the birth rate. A current example is Romania. The Romanian government has launched a campaign to increase its population from 22 million in 1984 to 25 million by 1990. The birth rate had been dropping rapidly, coinciding with a fall in living standards. In order to raise the birth rate, the government has made sure that contraception is unavailable, and has tightened the laws on abortion. The legal age of marriage for girls has been lowered to fifteen. Those men and women who have not married by the time they are twenty-five are being made to pay an extra 5 per cent income tax. The same applies to childless couples. Sterility treatment centres are to be set up to help those couples who experience difficulty in having children. Divorce is also to be made more difficult. All these measures are seen as ways of bolstering the family, therefore giving the maximum opportunity to have children.

Other governments have been concerned to limit the number of children born. In June 1984 the Singapore government offered to pay 5,000 dollars to every woman under thirty who agreed to be sterilized after the birth of her first or second child.

108

The conditions were that the families had to be of low income and of low education. This policy reflects the Singapore government's concern with the fact that uneducated women produce twice as many children as educated women. At the same time, educated women are being encouraged to marry educated men, and to look on motherhood as an alternative to a career. Here a government is clearly involving itself in family affairs as an act of social engineering.

The clearest contemporary example of state involvement in family life is probably China's one-child policy. The Chinese government wants to keep the population to under 1,200 million at the turn of the century. Failure to do this will stretch their resources to breaking point. China can probably comfortably support 700 million inhabitants. Extra mouths must mean lower living standards for all. The Chinese solution is to limit births to one child per couple.

The one-child policy is supervised by family planning committees in the local neighbourhood, and at the workplace. The family planning staff at the workplace involve themselves in the most personal affairs of the women workers. Women must seek permission to try to become pregnant, and there is often both a waiting list and a quota for the factory. Staff keep a record of contraception, of the woman's menstrual cycle, and watch for any maternal moods in the workers. Couples are encouraged to take out one-child certificates, a promise to have only one child. In return the couple get extra benefits, including free child health care and education, extra maternity leave, and higher family allowances. The child will also get priority in education and housing later in life.

Couples who break the agreement by having a second or third child suffer financial penalties. They have to repay the allowances they have been given, together with a fine on their wages. The couple will also risk losing their workplace bonuses. Women who become pregnant a second or third time come under tremendous pressure to have an abortion. Sterilization is encouraged so as to prevent accidents happening again.

Some couples try to fight the one-child policy. Chinese tradition stresses the need for a large family to help work the land and to support parents in old age. It is particularly important to the Chinese family that they have a son. Only boys can inherit the family name, and they are seen as better workers. In some villages the survival rate for baby boys was 25 per cent higher than for girls, the likely result of infanticide.

The governments of countries like Britain, France, and the United States do not appear to interfere so directly in family life as the Soviet or Chinese governments. But their policies nevertheless affect the role of families. It is the state that sets the legal framework of marriage and divorce. European countries with large Roman Catholic populations have restricted access to contraception and abortion.

The welfare policies that are introduced by governments mould the roles that families play. A good example of this can be seen in the way that the British government created a framework of nursery services during the Second World War. The nurseries were necessary in order to get as many women as possible working on the war effort. The government quickly set up 1,450 full-time nurseries for the children of working mothers. At the end of the war government policy was reversed, the nurseries were largely scrapped, and women were forced back into their domestic roles.

Over the last decade, the family has become a political issue in itself. This was made very clear in the period before the 1979 general election. Politicians argued over the relative merits of their policies for supporting the family. The protection of home, family, and children was seen as a vote-catcher. The Prime Minister, James Callaghan, was able to make the following statement in May 1978: 'Caring families are the basis of a society that cares .... If our people are grounded in a sound and sure family life, we will face change with a real chance of success.' Meanwhile, Conservative politicians were able to attack the Labour Chancellor of the Exchequer on the issue of child benefits, describing him as 'family-basher' Healey.

The family continues to be a political issue in Britain. The Conservative government of the 1980s argues that the family should be one of the main strengths of a healthy society. Political policies, such as the sale of council housing, and the privatization of health and education services, are seen as contributing to the independence of the family. Families are to be encouraged to help themselves rather than to become overdependent on the state. The care of the elderly should be within the family rather than in hospitals or local authority homes. Such policies are attractive to a government that is trying to cut public expenditure. The government assumes that the majority of the population lives in nuclear families capable of shouldering these responsibilities. Such policies also throw much of the strain of care on to the shoulders of women, pushing them back into domestic roles.

A similar political process has been at work in the United States. President Carter introduced a programme to protect the American family, based on ideas developed at his White House Conference on Families. The election of President Reagan brought more policies to support the family. There has now been a conservative backlash against liberal views on the family. A coalition of well-organized groups has led an attack on the abortion laws, the Equal Rights Amendment, on homosexuality, and on pornography. These problems were said to be damaging family life. The huge Reagan victory in the 1984 presidential election could see the introduction of policies to control abortion and support family life. Such policies would delight pressure groups such as the National Right to Life Committee, the National Pro-Family Coalition, and the Moral Majority.

The reproductive revolution

The rapid advances being made in reproductive technology

111

raise major moral issues for society. The first 'test-tube' baby, Louise Brown, was born at Oldham General Hospital in June 1978. Research into these new techniques has continued. More hospitals are putting the new techniques of reproductive technology into practice. These new techniques provide exciting opportunities but also raise major ethical, moral, and political issues. The political concern over the use of these methods led to the setting up of a committee to consider the issues involved. The Warnock Committee reported its findings in July 1984.

The distress caused by infertility prompted much of the research into the new techniques. The two key processes which make test-tube conceptions possible are In Vitro Fertilization (IVF) and Embryo Replacement (ER). The process involves the removal of a ripe egg from a woman, its fertilization in a glass vessel by sperm, and the replacement of the developing embryo into the woman.

Sociologists are interested in how society will face these issues. The dominant ideology of the family will have to adjust to these developments. Should IVF only be offered to heterosexual couples living in a stable relationship? Should a doctor be able to refuse this treatment to a single woman, or a homosexual couple? What is to stop doctors judging the suitability of a woman for IVF on social grounds, such as life style or political beliefs? Who is to give guidance to the medical profession?

A particular issue considered by the Warnock Committee was the possible use of surrogate mothers – fertile women who bear children for infertile couples. The surrogate mother could be fertilized by artificial insemination, or by sexual relations with the husband. The birth of the Cotton baby in January 1985 has made this possibility into a difficult moral and medical problem. The legal implications and the wide publicity has resulted in parliamentary attempts to control such developments. The government has been urged to introduce legislation that will outlaw surrogate pregnancies and prevent the development of commercial surrogacy agencies. Others have suggested that a way around such controls would be for women in the third world to act as surrogate mothers. Such womb leasing might then only cost about £1000. The Cotton case has shown how complicated are the issues surrounding the new reproductive technology.

The scientists conducting research in this field face specific moral problems. At what age should a fertilized embryo be seen as a potential human being? What should we feel about attempts to grow a baby outside the womb, or in the womb of a chimpanzee? Such developments are not all that far in the future – they are already being discussed.

The report of the Warnock Committee accepted the need to continue research into the problems of infertility, but rejected the idea of surrogate motherhood as a logical development of the use of IVF. The majority of the Warnock Committee wanted the operation of surrogate motherhood agencies to be a criminal offence. The report argues that their most important recommendation is to set up a statutory licensing authority, with a substantial lay membership, to regulate specific infertility services, and to control medical and scientific research that involves the use of human genetic material.

The developments in reproductive technology challenge some of our basic assumptions about the family and reproduction. The knowledge that has been developed cannot now be easily forgotten. Family life in one hundred years' time could be radically different from today. Sociology and the other social sciences may have some role to play in explaining how to approach the problems that this may create in society.

Capturing the middle ground

This book has tried to raise a range of academic and personal issues for the student new to the sociology of the family. It has presented material from a number of different areas. The interested student should now be in a better position to launch into the more detailed exploration of the vast range of writings on the family. The problem for the student is how to make sense of the different strands of social scientific, medical, and feminist research.

Sociologists are also members of families, and must grapple with the same personal search for satisfaction and happiness in their relationships. They are not immune from the conflicting emotions associated with love, marriage, parenthood, divorce, old age, and bereavement. This means that students are having to study an institution while at the same time finding their own personal identity in their own family.

A significant number of the readers of this book, the young people studying for their first examinations in sociology, will find themselves entering careers that involve working with families. Much of the professional life of social workers centres on trying to patch up the family problems of their clients. Social workers, teachers, counsellors, and the medical profession are all now taught how to use their professional expertise to intervene in family situations.

Sociologists are not, therefore, alone in having to solve the problems of relating their intellectual knowledge of the family to their own attempts to live a successful family life. Two American sociologists, Brigitte and Peter Berger, faced this problem in their recent book, *The War over The Family* (1983). They subtitled the book 'Capturing the middle ground'. It is an attempt to assess the merits of the various sociological and political debates over the family. They argue that it is necessary to build bridges between the various positions so that one can make progress from what they call the middle ground. Berger and Berger, in their conclusion, suggest six general principles which take account of sociological research but, at the same time, suggest ways that governments can cope with the needs of the family as an institution.

The first principle involves the recognition of the primacy of the family in the lives of individuals. The policy of the state should in no way harm the family. The concern of feminists with the rights of women should still allow individuals to recognize the central role of family life for all, but particularly for children.

114

The second principle advocates the restoration of the family as an area of private life. Berger and Berger believe that governments should adopt an attitude of 'benign neglect' where the style, the sexual morality, and the beliefs of individuals should be the internal private concern of families. Care should be taken to prevent more private matters becoming 'problematized' as public issues. This leads on to the problems and issues associated with their third principle, the need for the preservation of the autonomy of the family. One of the major issues facing the welfare systems in many countries is the feeling that the state is encroaching more and more on people's lives. Where should one draw the boundaries of state action?

A fourth principle argues that public policy on the family must take account of the pluralism of family types. There must be recognition that there is no one best or most natural form of family. Berger and Berger argue that such a principle does not conflict with their own belief in the values of the bourgeois family, a belief that they feel is shared by the great majority of people in western societies.

Their fifth principle is a plea for the restoration of parental rights. They argue that, in the majority of cases, parental wishes should take precedence over the views of the professional worker. The Bergers believe that, in most cases, the common sense of parents can be trusted. This is particularly important in such areas as education, where the middle-class views of the professional may conflict with the wishes of the parent.

The sixth and final principle echoes one of the major themes of British sociological studies of the family, the need to maintain community structures. Most families are embedded in larger communities which provide a mediating structure between the public and private worlds of family life. Public policy should try to support these communities as a way of helping to support the family.

These principles reflect the theoretical and cultural traditions which permeate the Berger's treatise on the family. Every reader must judge their worth according to their own sociological position and their own individual experience. But what they do try to achieve is a merger of the two sides of our experience of the family, the academic and the personal. The student of the sociology of the family must at some stage attempt to find his or her own 'middle ground'.

Further reading

Abrams and McCulloch (1975) provide an interesting sociological account of the commune movement in Britain. Rigby (1974) gives some good descriptive material on specific examples of communes. Recent material on the kibbutzim is scarce. The Family Policy Studies Centre (formerly the Study Commission on the Family) provides a number of reports that suggest possible policy requirements. Some of the best discussions of the implications of the new reproductive technology can be found in magazines linked to the women's movement, for instance Spare Rib *or* Trouble and Strife. *Finally, Berger and Berger (1983) is worth reading as an attempt to pull all the threads together, although not everyone will agree with their six principles for 'capturing the middle ground'.*

References

Abrams, P. and McCulloch, A. (1975) *Communes, Sociology and Society*. Cambridge: Cambridge University Press.

Althusser, L. (1971) *Lenin and Philosophy and Other Essays*. London: New Left Books.

Anderson, M. (1971) *Family Structure in Nineteenth Century Lancashire*. Cambridge: Cambridge University Press.

Anderson, M. (1980) *Approaches to the History of the Western Family, 1500–1914*. London: Macmillan.

Ariès, P. (1962) *Centuries of Childhood*. Harmondsworth: Penguin.

Ballard, R. (1982) South Asian Families. In R.N. Rapoport, M. Fogarty, and R. Rapoport (eds) *Families in Britain*. London: Routledge & Kegan Paul.

Banks, J. (1954) *Prosperity and Parenthood*. London: Routledge & Kegan Paul.

Barrow, J. (1982) West Indian Families: An Insider's Perspective. In R.N. Rapoport, M. Fogarty, and R. Rapoport (eds) *Families in Britain*. London: Routledge & Kegan Paul.

Bell, C. (1968) *Middle Class Families*. London: Routledge & Kegan Paul.

117

Bell, C. and Newby, H. (1971) *Community Studies*. London: George Allen & Unwin.

Berger, B. and Berger, P. (1983) *The War over the Family*. London: Hutchinson.

Bott, E. (1957) *Family and Social Network*. London: Tavistock.

Cooper, D. (1971) *The Death of the Family*. Harmondsworth: Penguin.

Creighton, S. (1984) *Trends in Child Abuse*. London: NSPCC.

Davidoff, L. (1973) *The Best Circles: Society, Etiquette and the Season*. London: Croom Helm.

Davidoff, L., L'Esperance, J. and Newby, H. (1976) Landscape with Figures: Home and Community in English Society. In J. Mitchell and A. Oakley, *The Rights and Wrongs of Women*. Harmondsworth: Penguin.

Delamont, S. (1980) *The Sociology of Women*. London: George Allen & Unwin.

Dennis, N., Henriques, F., and Slaughter, C. (1956) *Coal is Our Life*. London: Eyre & Spottiswoode.

Dobash, R.E. and Dobash, R. (1980) *Violence against Wives*. London: Open Books.

Driver, G. (1982) West Indian Families: An Anthropological Perspective. In R.N. Rapaport, M. Fogarty, and R. Rapoport (eds) *Families in Britain*. London: Routledge & Kegan Paul.

Engels, F. (1884) *The Origin of the Family, Private Property and the State*. London: Lawrence & Wishart.

Ermisch, J. (1983) *The Political Economy of Demographic Change*. London: Policy Studies Institute and Heinemann.

Fletcher, R. (1966) *The Family and Marriage in Britain*. Harmondsworth: Penguin.

Friedan, B. (1963) *The Feminist Mystique*. Harmondsworth: Penguin.

Gavron, H. (1966) *The Captive Wife*. Harmondsworth: Penguin.

Gettes, R. (1979) *Family Violence*. Beverly Hills, Calif.: Sage.

Gittins, D. (1982) *Fair Sex: Family Size and Structure 1900–39*. London: Hutchinson.

Gomm, R. (1981) Chapter on Population. In P. McNeil and C. Townley (eds) *Fundamentals of Sociology*. London: Hutchinson.

Goode, W.J. (1963) *World Revolution and Family Patterns*. New York: Free Press.

Gordon, M. (1972) *The Nuclear Family in Crisis*. London: Harper & Row.

118

Gough, E. (1959) Is the family universal? The Nayar Case. In N.W. Bell and E.F. Vogel, (eds) *A Modern Introduction to the Family*. London, Collier-Macmillan.

Gowler, D. and Legge, K. (1982) Dual-worker Families. In R.N. Rapoport, M. Fogarty, and R. Rapoport (eds) *Families in Britain*. London: Routledge & Kegan Paul.

Harris, C. (1983) *The Family and Industrial Society*. London: George Allen & Unwin.

Hawthorne, G. (1970) *The Sociology of Fertility*. London: Collier-Macmillan.

Irvine, E. (1980) *The Family in the Kibbutz*. London: Study Commission on the Family.

Jackson, B. (1982) Single-parent Families. In R.N. Rapoport, M. Fogarty, and R. Rapoport (eds) *Families in Britain*. London: Routledge & Kegan Paul.

Jackson, B. (1984) *Fatherhood*. London: George Allen & Unwin.

Kerr, M. (1958) *The People of Ship Street*. London: Routledge & Kegan Paul.

Khan, V. (ed.) (1979) *Minority Families in Britain*. London: Macmillan.

Kitzinger, S. (1978) *Women as Mothers*. London: Fontana.

Laing, R.D. (1971) *Politics and the Family*. London: Macmillan.

Laslett, P. (1965) *The World We Have Lost*. London: Methuen.

Laslett, P. (1977) *Family Life and Illicit Love in Earlier Generations*. London: Methuen.

Laslett, P. (1983) *The World We Have Lost – Further Explored*. London: Methuen.

Leach, E. (1967) Ourselves and Others, Third Reith Lecture. In *The Listener*, 30 November, London.

Leach, E. (1982) In the *Observer*, 7 October, London.

Lee, R. (1979) *Communes as Alternative Families*. M. Phil. thesis of North-East London Polytechnic.

Leonard, D. (1980) *Sex and Generation*. London: Tavistock.

McCulloch, A. (1982) Alternative Households. In R.N. Rapoport, M. Fogarty, and R. Rapoport (eds) *Families in Britain*. London: Routledge & Kegan Paul.

Marsden, D. and Owens, D. (1975) The Jekyll and Hyde Marriages. *New Society*, 8 May.

Mead, M. (1943) *Coming of Age in Samoa*. Harmondsworth: Penguin.

Mead, M. (1962) *Male and Female*. Harmondsworth: Penguin.

119

Mead, M. (1963) *Growing Up in New Guinea*. Harmondsworth: Penguin.

Morgan, D. (1975) *Social Theory and the Family*. London: Routledge & Kegan Paul.

Murdock, G. P. (1949) *Social Structure*. New York: Macmillan.

Myrdal, A. and Klein, V. (1956) *Women's Two Roles*. London: Routledge & Kegan Paul.

Oakley, A. (1972) Are Husbands Good Housewives? *New Society*, 17 February.

Oakley, A. (1974a) *Housewife*. Harmondsworth: Penguin.

Oakley, A. (1974b) *The Sociology of Housework*. Oxford: Martin Robertson.

Oakley, A. (1979) *Becoming a Mother*. Oxford: Martin Robertson.

Oakley, A. (1982) *Subject Women*. London: Fontana.

Oakley, R. (1982) Cypriot Families. In R.N. Rapoport, M. Fogarty, and R. Rapoport (eds) *Families in Britain*. London: Routledge & Kegan Paul.

Parker, R. (1982) Family and Social Policy: An Overview. In R.N. Rapoport, M. Fogarty, and R. Rapoport (eds) *Families in Britain*. London: Routledge & Kegan Paul.

Parsons, T. and Bales, R. (1956) *Family, Socialization and Interaction Process*. London: Routledge & Kegan Paul.

Pearsall, R. (1969) *The Worm in the Bud*. Harmondsworth: Penguin.

Pizzey, E. (1974) *Scream Quietly or the Neighbours Will Hear*. Harmondsworth: Penguin.

Popay, J., Rimmer, L., and Rossiter, C. (1983) *One-Parent Families*. London: Study Commission on the Family.

Rapoport, R.N., Fogarty, M., and Rapoport, R. (eds) (1982) *Families in Britain*. London: Routledge & Kegan Paul.

Rapoport, R.N. and Rapoport, R. (1976) *Dual-Career Families Re-examined*. London: Martin Robertson.

Rapoport, R. and Rapoport, R.N., with Bumstead, J. (1978) *Working Couples*. London: Routledge & Kegan Paul.

Rees, A. (1950) *Life in a Welsh Countryside*. Cardiff: University of Wales Press.

Rigby, A. (1974) *Alternative Realities*. London: Routledge & Kegan Paul.

Rosser, K. and Harris, C. (1965) *The Family and Social Change*. London: Routledge & Kegan Paul.

Shorter, E. (1976) *The Making of the Modern Family*. London: Collins.

Smelser, N. (1982) The Victorian Family. In R.N. Rapoport, M. Fogarty, and R. Rapoport (eds) *Families in Britain*. London: Routledge & Kegan Paul.

Stanway, A. (1980) *Why Us? A Common-sense Guide for the Childless*. St Albans: Mayflower.

Townsend, P. (1957) *The Family Life of Old People*. Harmondsworth: Penguin.

Tunstall, J. (1962) *The Fisherman*. London: MacGibbon & Kee.

Turner, C. (1969) *The Family and Kinship in Modern Britain*. London: Routledge & Kegan Paul.

Williams, W. (1956) *The Sociology of an English Village*. London: Routledge & Kegan Paul.

Williams, W. (1963) *Ashworthy*. London: Routledge & Kegan Paul.

Willmott, P. and Young, M. (1957) *Family and Kinship in East London*. London: Routledge & Kegan Paul.

Willmott, P. and Young, M. (1960) *Family and Class in a London Suburb*. London: Routledge & Kegan Paul.

Willmott, P. and Young, M. (1973) *The Symmetrical Family*. London: Routledge & Kegan Paul.

Index

hold numbers and trends 66–71; large scale surveys in 33–6; marriage in 71–3; parenthood in 73–4; sex and generation survey 33, 37–40; state and family 107, 110–11; violence in 89; welfare state 98–9, 107, 110; *see also* changing British families

Brown, L. 112

Callaghan, J. 110
Cambridge Group for History of Population and Social Structure 43, 46
Carter, J. 111
capitalism, family as tool of 26–8
changing British families 45–68; pre-industrial 45, 46–8, 63, 74; industrialization and change 48–50, 63; Victorian era 50–4; demographic and social change at turn of century 54–9; post-war sociology 59–64; *see also* Britain
changing shape of family 2–6, 7, 21, 25; cultural differences in forms 5–6, 46–8, 115; development cycle 3–5; historical 2–3; industrialization and 48–54; turn of century 54–9; post-war 54–9
childhood, length of 3, 11–12
childlessness 73–4, 87, 108, 112–13
children: abuse of 90–4; in alternative families 17–18, 103–04, 106; changing attitude to 54–5; death of 42, 47, 54, 92, 94, 110; and divorce 88; numbers of 47; in one-parent families 70; prostitution 52; rearing and support 4, 10,

21, 22–3, 28, 103–04, 106; roles 30, 53; socialization of 4, 10, 25, 30; stress 29–30, 88; working 53; *see also* birth; parents
China, one-child policy in 109–10
class: and age of mother at birth of child 73; and family forms 51; and roles 60, 62–4, 75; and violence 93–4; *see also* middle class; working class
cohabitation 72, 95
collective households 103, 105–06
conjugal roles *see* husband-wife
communes 104–06
community: identity 103; life 16–18, 102–06; structure, maintenance of 115
comparative studies, 5–6, 46, 47–8, 115
conflict 77; *see also* violence
consciousness, false 28
contraception 55–7, 97, 108–09
convergence of family forms 63
Cooper, D. 29
costs *see* economic/s
Cotton case 112–13
courtship, study of 33, 37–40
Creighton, S. 91–3
crisis in family: breakdown 3, 4; *see also* death; divorce; elderly, caring for 98–100, 111; one-parent families 70, 77, 86, 94–8; violence 89–94
cultural differences 5–6, 46–8, 78–81, 111
Cypriot families 79

Davidoff, L. 51–2
death/mortality: age at 47; of children 42, 47, 54, 92, 96, 110; rates 41, 42, 47, 49, 54,

Marx, K. 1
Marxism 1, 26–8
Mead, M. 6
men: age at marriage 71–2;
    domestic tasks 64, 77–8; in
    one-parent families 70–1;
    role, dominant 1, 26, 40, 51,
    63, 78–80, 95–6; *see also*
    husband-wife; parents
middle class: age of mother 73;
    children 55; education 58;
    roles 62; study of 33, 34–5,
    62; Victorian 51–2; violence
    94; women 25; *see also* class
migration 49, 78–81
Morgan, D. 18, 31
mortality *see* death
mothers *see* women
Murdock, G. P. 21
Myrdal, A. 14

National Society for Prevention
    of Cruelty to Children 91–4
Nayar of Kerala 14–16
Newby, H. 44, 65
Noyes, J. H. 16–18
nuclear family 8–9, 21; func-
    tionalist view of 21–3; house-
    holds 67; instability 46; iso-
    lated 30–1; pre-industrial 48
nurseries 76, 110
nutrition 46

Oakley, A. 14, 24–5, 65, 77–8
Oakley, R. 79, 100
obligations 7–8, 50, 60
Office of Population Censuses
    and Surveys 42
old age *see* elderly
one-parent families 70, 94–8;
    poverty 77, 86
one-person households 68–9
Oneida Community 16–18
Open University 40

Owens, D. 89

Pacific Island cultures 6
parents 73–4; relationship with
    children 11–12, 50, 104; res-
    toration of rights 115; *see also*
    children; death; men; women
Parker, R. 13
Parsons, T. 20–2
part-time work 77
patriarchalism *see* men, role
Pearsall, R. 52
perinatal mortality 42, 96
physical support 10, 20
Pizzey, E. 100
pluralism of family types 115;
    see also alternative
political issue, family as 110–11
Popay, J. 95
population explosion 49; *see
    also* demographic
post-war sociology of family
    59–64
poverty 77, 86; *see also* eco-
    nomic/s
pre-industrial families 25, 26,
    45, 46–8, 63, 74
primacy of family 114
privacy 30–1, 49, 115
procreation *see* reproduction
prostitution 52
psychology, radical 29–31
puberty 46

qualitative data 36, 37
quantitative data 33–6

radical psychology 29–31
Rapoport, R. N. and R. 14, 65,
    81, 100
Reagan, R. 111
recreation 10
Rees, A. 64
relationships in family 11–14,

surrogate mothers 112–13
surveys *see* studying
Swansea, surveys in 33, 37–40, 62–3
symmetrical families 63–4; study of 34, 35–6, 63–4

'test-tube' babies 112
theoretical approaches to family 20–31; feminist 23–6, 27, 28, 30; functionalism 20–3, 30; Marxist 26–8; radical psychology 29–31
time 2–4, 25, 35; *see also* historical
Tunstan, J. 61
Turner, C. 3

unemployment 93–4
United States: family in 21–2, 111; Oneida Community in 16–18; violence in 89
urban areas 49, 63

Victorian Britain 50–4
violence 89–94; battered wives 89–90; child abuse 90–4

Warnock Report (1984) 112, 113
welfare state *see* social services
West Indian families 80
wife *see* husband-wife; women
Williams, W. 64
Willmott, P. and Young, M. 9, 33–6, 43–4; on family and class in London suburb 33, 34–5, 62; on family and kinship in East London 23,

33, 34, 60; on symmetrical family 35–6, 63–4
women: age at marriage 71–2; battered 89–90; demographic change and 57; domestic role of 23–4, 27–8, 40, 59, 107; education of 52, 58; elderly, caring for 13; fertility 41–2, 46–7, 49, 54, 68; as heads of families 70–1, 80, 95; and illegitimacy 70, 87, 95, 96–8; infertility treatments 112–13; invisible 24–5; legislation for equality 57–8; and marriage 14, 25, 39–40; mother-daughter relationships 14, 60–3; one-parent family heads 70–1; relationships with husbands *see* husband-wife; roles in family 6, 11–14, 21, 23–7, 40, 51–2, 57–9, 78–80; roles in society 24–5; self-image 30, 90; socialization of 95; sociologists 37, 38; surrogate mothers 112–13; working 14, 27, 52–3, 57–9, 63–4, 74–8; *see also* birth; children; feminism; parents
work *see* labour; women, working
working class: age of mother 73; children 55; contraception 56–7; roles in family 13–14, 60–3; socialization of 28; studies of 23, 33, 34, 60; Victorian 51, 52–3; violence 93–4; women 14

Young, *see* Willmott and Young
young people 12, 96–7; *see also* children